The Kogan Page Practical Trainer Series

Series Editor: Roger Buckley

Competence-Based Assessment Techniques Shirley Fletcher
Cost-Effective Training Tony Newby
Designing Competence-Based Training Shirley Fletcher
Effective Feedback Skills Tim Russell
How to Design and Deliver Equal Opportunities Training Judith Taylor and Helen Garrett
How to Design and Deliver Quality Service Training Tony Newby
How to Design and Deliver Retirement Training Marcella Bailey and Peter Reynolds
How to Design and Introduce Appraisal Training Carol McCallum
How to Design and Introduce Trainer Development Programmes Leslie Rae
How to Introduce Target Setting Richard Hale
How to Take a Training Audit Michael Applegarth
How to Write and Prepare Training Materials Nancy Stimson
The In-House Trainer as Consultant Mike Saunders and Keith Holdaway
The Lone Trainer Mike Saunders and Keith Holdaway
Management Development Outdoors Bill Krouwel and Steve Goodwill
Managing Training Sunny Stout
Marketing the Training Function Joyce Levant and David Cleeton
One-to-One Training and Coaching Skills Roger Buckley and Jim Caple
A Practical Approach to Group Training David Leigh
Quality and Competence Shirley Fletcher
Selecting and Using Training Aids David Flegg and Josephine McHale
Training for Total Quality Management David R Jeffries, Bill Evans and Peter Reynolds
Training Needs Analysis in the Workplace Robyn Peterson
Validating Your Training Tony Newby

How to Design and Deliver Induction Training Programmes

UMETLD

PRACTICAL TRAINER SERIES

How to Design and Deliver Induction Training Programmes

SECOND EDITION

MICHAEL MEIGHAN

KOGAN
PAGE

To Jill, Christopher and Catriona

First published in 1991

Reprinted 1992

This second edition published in 1995

Kogan Page Limited
120 Pentonville Road
London N1 9JN

© Michael Meighan, 1991, 1995

British Library Cataloguing in Publication Data

A CIP record for this book is available from the British Library.

ISBN 0 7494 1667 X

Typeset by Saxon Graphics Limited, Derby
Printed and bound in Great Britain by Biddles Ltd, Guildford and Kings Lynn

Contents

Series Editor's Foreword   9

Preface to the Second Edition   10

PART 1: HOW TO DESIGN INDUCTION TRAINING PROGRAMMES

1   Why Have Induction?   13

Case Studies of Ineffective Induction   13
The Benefits of Induction   17

2   Who Should Receive Induction Training?   29

Different Categories of Newcomer   30
Job Handovers   43

3   What Shape Should Induction Take?   47

Case Studies of Poor Induction Programmes   47
A Model Induction Programme   50

4   Designing an Induction Training Programme   63

'Must Knows', 'Should Knows' and 'Could Knows'   64
Aims and Objectives   65
Designing the Training   68
The Use of National Standards   72
Designing to Standards   74

PART 2: DELIVERING INDUCTION TRAINING
PROGRAMMES   77

5 **Methods of Delivering Induction Training Programmes**   **79**

   Learner-centred Methods   79
   Delivering to Standards   83

6 **Skills, Knowledge and Attitudes for Delivering Induction
   Programmes**   **86**

   Skills, Knowledge and Attitudes Required   86
   Key Skills for Delivering Induction   88

7 **Roles in Induction – Who Carries it Out?**   **94**

   Roles in Induction   94

8 **Induction as Part of a Process**   **99**

   The Employment Cycle   99
   A New Entrant Scheme   106

9 **New Issues in Induction**   **108**

   New Approaches in Training and Development   108
   Quality Initiatives   114
   Conclusion   115

Appendix 1. A Sample Induction Training Course Programme   **117**

Appendix 2. Checklist for Planning a Training Course   **123**

Select Bibliography   **126**

Index   **128**

Series Editor's Foreword

Organizations get things done when people do their jobs effectively. To make this happen they need to be well trained. A number of people are likely to be involved in this training by identifying the needs of the organization and of the individual, by selecting or designing appropriate training to meet those needs, by delivering it and by assessing how effective it was. It is not only 'professional' or full-time trainers who are involved in this process: personnel managers, line managers, supervisors and job holders are all likely to have a part to play.

This series has been written for all those who get involved with training in some way or another, whether they are senior personnel managers trying to link the goals of the organization with training needs or job holders who have been given responsibility for training newcomers. Therefore, the series is essentially a practical one which focuses on specific aspects of the training function. This is not to say that the theoretical underpinnings of the practical aspects of training are unimportant. Anyone seriously interested in training is strongly encouraged to look beyond 'what to do' and 'how to do it' and to delve into the areas of why things are done in a particular way.

The authors have been selected because they have considerable practical experience. All have shared, at some time, the same difficulties, frustrations and satisfactions of being involved in training and are now in a position to share with others some helpful and practical guidelines.

In this book, Michael Meighan provides guidelines on how to design effective induction training. There is more to induction than merely 'showing newcomers the ropes'. Newcomers could include those entering the world of work for the first time, those returning to work after career breaks, those who have been retrained in new skills and those who are moving from one department to another. They all have their particular training and orientation needs; similarly the organization has a need to motivate them and to gain their commitment and loyalty. All of this can be achieved only by a well-presented induction programme.

ROGER BUCKLEY

Preface to the Second Edition

When I first wrote this book it was based on my experience that proper induction is fundamental to both the retention of, and development of staff, not simply for the benefit of these new members of staff but also because induction can have a major influence on the development of a business – it is the start of a longer process that leads on to staff appraisal and systematic staff training and development.

At that time my approach was one of 'best practice' in that there were no specific requirements or recommendations for organizations to implement induction programmes. However, over the past few years a number of initiatives have emerged that make the use of induction programmes even more necessary, not only in terms of good practice but because they are now required for specific purposes.

This revised edition of the book introduces these initiatives. The first, in which there is a specific requirement for induction, is Investors In People (IIP). IIP is a government-sponsored award that now requires organizations working towards the award to implement systematic induction for all staff. The introduction of the new National and Scottish Vocational Qualifications calls for proper inductions not just for new staff but for the large numbers of existing staff who may be working towards these qualifications. The movement towards empowerment, mentoring and 'the learning organization', which are explained in this text, also means systematic implementation through communication with new and existing staff. So too does the general movement towards quality awards such as BS5750/ISO9000, which require staff to be trained in quality management and control. This clearly should be tackled at the induction stage.

A number of other issues have now been included for the first time in this new edition such as providing induction for staff who are travelling abroad and growing emphasis on continuing induction for staff moving within the organization or taking up qualifications.

It is clear that the original concept was right and it is evident through the above initiatives that the place of induction is now fully recognized. This book continues to be a framework for systematic induction training programmes that will meet all of these needs.

MICHAEL MEIGHAN

Part 1 HOW TO DESIGN INDUCTION TRAINING PROGRAMMES

1 Why Have Induction?

▷   CHAPTER SUMMARY   ◁

Systematic induction to the organization is often ignored and results in a range of benefits being missed:

- Financial. An unnecessarily large turnover costs more in recruitment.
- Motivational. Staff who undergo quality induction training programmes are more likely to give longer-term commitment to the organization.
- Training and Development. As induction is possibly the first experience the newcomer has to the organization's approach to training it is important that it makes a good impression.
- Monitoring the external environment. Newcomers can be an effective gauge of how the organization is perceived externally.
- Influencing present staff. Induction can have a beneficial effect on present staff through their involvement in the process.
- Induction can make a contribution to the implementation of quality systems.

Case Studies of Ineffective Induction

Carol was seventeen. A young woman who had left school unqualified but who had achieved some qualifications and experience on a government training programme while working in a local solicitor's office.

Moving on to a large accountancy practice she met a completely different environment and a new set of people. For the very first time she found herself working in the harsh reality of commercial pressures and conflicting demands on her time and abilities.

Carol had never before had more than one boss, and she could not get the hang of the new equipment and systems. Not only that, but there didn't seem to be anyone she could confide in as they all seemed to be too busy working to take much notice of her. It all caused her a great deal of distress. Luckily she met her old manager who offered her her job back at the solicitor's. So she accepted the job and wrote the accountancy practice off as a bad experience. She would just stay where she was from now on and make the most of it, even though the money wasn't very good.

Gerry was a time-served and qualified electrical fitter who had had only one employer. Unfortunately he had been laid off a couple of years ago when the company he worked for went into liquidation. Always a worrier, he suffered badly in the first year with nervous depression which wasn't helped very much by the break-up of his marriage. After a great deal of help from doctors and counsellors, and also from a college course in computing technology which boosted his morale considerably, he was offered a job as a planning technician with an oil company. Some of this work was offshore and he looked forward to it with some trepidation but also with excitement.

Unfortunately Gerry was disappointed. The work he was expected to do was menial and did not take into account his experience and qualifications. Neither did it involve the offshore work he was led to believe it would. Not only that, but he found his immediate boss was abrasive, and dismissive of the personnel section who had employed Gerry. When he asked whether he was to get any further training, his boss's reaction was 'Do you think we employed you to send you to university?' Gerry left the same night. That was several months ago and Gerry is still unemployed, with few immediate prospects because of his poor work record and his mental state which has now deteriorated.

Alex was an ex-teacher who had retired early from the profession. He had enough for himself and his wife to retire on and still live in the fashion to which they had become accustomed. However, with the collapse of a major investment company, Alex lost a large proportion of the lump sum he had received on retirement. Now he had to go back to work in order to keep enough aside for the next five years until he was 65, when he would be eligible for a state pension.

His first step was to approach the employment service who referred him to a government training scheme, where on the first day he found himself sitting in a crowded college room with about 25 other people of various ages. Someone he could not hear properly, both because of his slight hearing problem and because he was at the back of the room, was trying to explain about the 'Return to Work' programme.

Looking around him, Alex could see a variety of people. Obviously a lot of them were unemployed. Some were young, from about 18 upwards. With horror he recognized at least two boys whom he had taught and who had given him difficulty at school. Were they to be on the same retraining programme as him? The thought appalled him. They hadn't seen him because he came in at the back just as the session was about to start. At the first opportunity, when the lecturer started a video which he couldn't see or hear anyway, Alex got up and left.

Alex was a few weeks unemployed before a head-teacher phoned him up to ask whether he was interested in some temporary teaching because of the present shortage of teachers. Alex now does enough work not to have to touch any of his savings, and actively discourages anyone from going on government training schemes.

Simon was a recent graduate with a degree in geology. He had been working for six months on a research project for a large oil company when he was sent, with another new colleague, to an oil base in North Africa. He had never been in a hot climate before and although he was well prepared in terms of passports and visas, he and his colleagues were both unprepared for the fact that once they had arrived at the airport, he would have to drive 200 miles overland to reach his base. Halfway there, overcome with heat and fatigue and while his colleague was sleeping, he fell asleep at the wheel and crashed. He was lucky to escape with minor injuries as they were quickly spotted by another vehicle on an otherwise lonely road. After treatment and recuperation, Simon decided that he did not again want to put his life in the hands of the oil company and found another job at home.

Are These Your Experiences of Induction?

These four stories are all based on fact and are clearly extremely sad – and in the last case potentially dangerous. I bet, though, when you read them, that although they may not be related to your field, they nevertheless rang some bells. What is the common factor in these stories? Not the fact that they were all unemployed, because that was not the case. They were not all suffering from the same problem or needs. They had different work experience and there was a wide variation in age. No, the common bond was that they were embarking on new careers or jobs with new organizations and were grossly mishandled, causing them to condemn the whole organization on the basis of a few people who, if they had had the right skills, knowledge and attitudes, could not only have retained these new entrants but could have brought their organization and themselves more credibility and respect.

It should not stretch your imagination very far to go back in time to remember when you were disappointed with a new job, to when you were treated poorly by staff you were looking forward to working with. Did the expectations raised by an interviewer or recruiter not meet the reality of the job? Were you ever in a position when all you wanted to do was get out and forget the job?

Perhaps this might seem to be a very jaundiced way of looking at how people start a new occupation or training or educational course. Possibly it is a bit negative. Possibly you have not had experiences like Carol, Gerry, Alex or Simon. Possibly you are one of the lucky ones. Because it is a reality that a poor introduction to an occupation, whether it be to training, to work, or to college has a demotivating effect on many people.

Table 1.1 shows a list of the kind of stresses experienced by someone taking up a new career. Think about these stresses in relation to your own experiences. Are any of them familiar?

Table 1.1 *Stress checklist*

Changing job or career	new colleagues to work with new bosses new environment new skills to learn	new rules to follow new directions travelling abroad
Moving house	moving to new area choosing the house arranging the finance change of school for children educational standards to maintain	comparability of house partner's career to consider the physical move selling the old house
Promotion	new responsibilities bigger budgets	a first-time manager?

Was The New Organization Supportive?

If you experienced any of the above, how were you helped to cope?

- Did the new organization help you fully during the change?
- Was the change compounded by difficulties at home?
- Were there financial difficulties?
- Did you have to move home?
- How did the new organization react to these difficulties?
- Were they sympathetic?
- Did they take any action or help out?
- Were you disappointed in the way you were treated?
- How did the way you were treated colour your first impressions of the organization, the job and the people?

- Did the new organization take into account your experience, qualifications, status, level of ability?
- Did the new organization give you enough information about the job and about the organization itself?
- Did the organization fully brief you if you had to travel abroad?

All too often, if we have been employed in a secure position for a number of years, it is easy to forget the difficulties faced by people who are new to an organization. This book is intended to remind all those involved in the induction of new entrants of those difficulties, and how properly organized induction can bring a whole range of benefits to the organization. But what are the benefits?

EXAMPLE OF GOOD PRACTICE

A multinational company with operations worldwide recognizes that staff new to the organization may need a great deal of support to begin with. They have appointed a welfare officer whose job it is to keep in regular contact with these staff to assist in any difficulties that they may experience; for example, house purchase, difficulties in schooling or in understanding currency. In one instance they were able to expedite flights in order to fly a staff member home to her sick daughter. This sort of support takes pressure off staff who are already under the pressure of learning a new job.

The Benefits of Induction

I believe there are six major benefits of a properly introduced and systematic approach to the induction of new staff:

1. Good induction can cut down recruitment costs.
2. Good induction can be a motivating factor for new staff.
3. Induction can be used as an introduction to the benefits of training and development.
4. The organization can learn from new staff.
5. Induction can have a beneficial effect on existing staff.
6. Induction can make a contribution to quality initiatives such as Investors In People.

Financial Benefits

Clearly, the level at which a firm recruits will determine the amount of money which is spent on recruitment. Also, the more professional the approach, the more money will be spent on advertising, interviewing and in-depth selection techniques.

In every static company, that is, one not expanding or contracting, the amount spent on recruitment will be directly proportional to staff turnover. That is, the higher the turnover rate, the higher will be the recruitment budget.

Managers can measure staff turnover over set periods using the formula in Table 1.2.

Table 1.2 *Staff turnover rate*

$$\frac{\text{number of leavers}}{\text{average number employed}} \times 100 = \text{turnover rate}$$

$$\text{e.g.} \quad \frac{12}{\frac{64 + 56}{2}} \times 100 = 20\%$$

Where 64 = number employed at beginning of period
56 = number employed at end of period
20 = average turnover rate per period

If a personnel or manpower section can detail the amount it spends on advertising and recruiting over the same period or if it can specify the costs of recruiting those personnel who leave, then we can get a measure of what it costs the company to lose staff against what it costs to recruit them. In my experience, few organizations go to the bother of making such comparisons, probably because of the difficulty in collecting statistics. Possibly they do not see it as a problem which can be solved through the collection of figures.

Also, in many cases, staff turnover is not seen to be related to induction of new staff. The question is, does it have to be? In many cases possibly not, as staff can leave for a number of reasons: they may well be going to better paid jobs; they may be leaving the area with their families; there may be better conditions and prospects elsewhere.

However, unless some sort of analysis is carried out to determine both the volume of staff leaving and why they leave, we cannot determine how best to keep them. Also it is very difficult to relate the fact that someone is leaving to go to a better paid job after a year to the fact that the employee did not undergo proper induction which met his or her needs and committed him or her to the organization. One way of finding out to what extent leavers leave because their initial aspirations have not been met is through exit interviewing, which we shall be looking at in Chapter 8. If exit interviews are carried out in a competent manner and linked into an initial induction programme and to continuous appraisal, we can go a long way towards finding out to what extent the organization has let the individual down. People do not always leave jobs or courses arbitrarily. It is often because they are disillusioned and let down, mishandled or misinformed. And it is always easy to blame leavers for not sticking at the job rather than ourselves or the organization for not keeping staff.

If an employee says he or she is leaving, whether it is after three weeks or three years, then we have to ask 'Why? What have I not done to retain this employee?' Or, more important, 'What have I done to discourage?' 'Have I not paid enough?' 'Have I allowed enough scope?' The answers might show that the person is leaving because prospects are better elsewhere and you cannot help in that direction. They might show that he or she is leaving for better money which you cannot provide.

If you have trained that person well and both you and the leaver have benefited from the training, you should be content that you have provided an opportunity for that individual to make progress rather than feel cheated that a well-trained member of staff has decided to leave. I have always taken it as a compliment if one of my staff has left for a better job. The leaver will always be an ambassador for you, your organization and your philosophy towards recruitment, training and development. However, if staff are leaving because you can't pay to retain them, then decisions may have to be made about this, and there should be a channel for communicating this information to senior managers and to the personnel section. I shall argue later on for a management information system which relates recruitment to induction and to staff appraisal and review, and finally to exit from the organization.

Of course, much of the above applies to larger organizations which may have to depend on formal systems to obtain information about leavers. However, the financial considerations apply just as much to the small organization as to the large. It may be more obvious in the small organization when staff leave and possibly more financially damaging, especially if staff with expert knowledge leave to go to competitors. Personnel journals are now talking of loyalty clauses and court cases to stop such poaching. This is a bit pointless as staff will stay if they want to, rather than if you want them to.

Therefore an organization should make them want to stay. Money does not always motivate, as I will try to explain later. What motivates, among other things, are good conditions and a good working environment, good leadership, and recognition. These things must all start with induction and be followed through. The argument is that financially we have to ask, 'Are we wasting money by not having a fully understood, comprehensive programme of inducting new entrants?'

A good induction system not only commits an individual to an organization. It can show that an organization is committed to the individual. It can ensure that any barriers to proper integration are identified right away. It can show that the organization cares for individuals. Having recruited them, you want to show that you want them to stay, and that you will do all in your power to retain them as long as they are doing their jobs competently. Financially it makes sense for every organization, whether this is seen in direct savings in personnel, recruitment or administration costs, or in indirect savings through having the reputation of being a good organization to work with.

Consider the figures in Table 1.3.

Table 1.3 *Recruiting costs*

John Smith – Electronic Engineer c. £17000.00

Cost of recruitment

	£
Advertisements – national press	1000.00
Expenses for candidates	1000.00
Psychometric testing	1200.00
Interviewers' salaries for time spent	600.00
Administration costs	200.00
Training costs	1000.00
Total costs	5000.00
Left after two months to go to another post.	
Cost of replacement (all the above)	5000.00

As you can see, the cost of recruiting an electronic engineer has worked out at about £10,000. It might be unusual for such a well paid employee to leave after such a short time. However it does happen. At the lower end of the salary scale turnover might be expected to be higher, especially in areas where it is easy to pick up jobs. The more new staff that are being recruited the more it is therefore going to cost to recruit replacements. It can get to the stage when some managers' time seems to be given over more to recruiting casual, part-time or full-time staff rather than to actually managing them. It is when this is happening that an organization should take stock and look at the cost of recruitment and selection as a percentage of overheads and ask whether this overhead could be reduced by the introduction of an induction system which takes account of turnover and reasons for it. It should really want to know why its staff are leaving. Later on we shall look at methods of finding out exactly why staff are leaving.

Motivational Benefits

I remember hearing a story some time ago concerning the American chief executive of a multinational company who was doing a whistlestop tour of his offices in Great Britain. Catching a clerk apparently with nothing to do and with no explanation why, he told the manager of the office: 'Sack that man and sell his desk'.

I have often wondered what was the turnover in that organization and the costs related to it. I wonder, too, what was the morale of the staff in his company. This is a classic case of blaming individuals for the ills of an organization, and frankly it isn't a good marketing strategy if you want to attract staff.

Some theories of motivation

There are several schools of thought in this area and which school you belong to is probably to do with what you feel about people in general and your staff in particular. This probably affects whether you will want to bother with induction or whether you will see it as an unnecessary luxury.

The Douglas McGregor X and Y theories

Douglas McGregor of the Massachusetts Institute of Technology, an organizational scientist well known in this field, had a theory about how people are treated in organizations: the X Manager and the Y Manager. According to McGregor, the X Manager believes:

1. People are inherently against work and will avoid it at all costs.
2. People have to be pushed and coerced to achieve productivity.
3. Human beings avoid responsibility.
4. Human beings are not ambitious.

The Y Manager believes that:

1. We naturally want to work.
2. We are satisfied by rewards rather than punishment.
3. We are ambitious, creative and will seek responsibility and control.

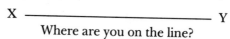

X ——————————————— Y

Where are you on the line?

In reality X managers would have to be at the extreme end of a line from Y managers. The question is, where do you as a manager, trainer, teacher, or leader lie on the line? I have to confess that my experience shows me that Y managers do get the best out of people. Because if you allow people to grow, then they will, and they will respect you for it. Occasionally I have come across a member of staff who has taken severe advantage of my goodwill. Fortunately this has not caused me to tar everyone with the same brush. If our pride is hurt because we have been suckered once or twice and it makes us become X managers then the respect others have for us will suffer in the long term.

The point is that if you want a prospective employee to grow and develop, to take responsibility, and act on initiative, then you have to show from an early stage that you will help him or her do these things. The place to do this is on an induction programme. It can be done by showing examples of how this is possible. Case studies of successful staff at every level can be used. You could possibly introduce such staff on induction courses. You could let newcomers see how the organization treats and responds to staff through the staff suggestion scheme or bonus scheme perhaps. But quite decidedly don't tell them how wonderful your company is as they may not believe you unless you can prove it: and of course you may be wrong. It's amazing how many managers, owners, senior staff, salesmen and training staff think that their organizations are wonderful. Unfortunately lesser but more informed mortals on the shop floor or back at base may have a very different opinion, and these are the ones who have to follow through. Therefore don't make promises that your organization cannot follow up.

Better still, why not check what information your staff get at induction against whether the organization can come up with the goods. For example there isn't much point in saying how wonderful promotion prospects are if people in the organization believe that promotion is based on factors other than good personnel practice.

This aspect of checking whether the induction course or training programme is effective is called evaluation and is extremely important in ensuring that the programme is meeting the needs of the organization.

Frederick Hertzberg's two-factor theory

Professor Frederick Hertzberg came up with the 'Two-Factor' theory of motivation. He said that there are a number of things at work which make us unhappy and a number of things which motivate us. The things which can make us unhappy he called the 'Hygiene' factors and are such things as salaries, conditions, supervision and the people we work with. By improving conditions or salaries, says Hertzberg, we may be making people more satisfied. However that doesn't mean that we are going to be more motivated to work. Motivation comes through the 'Motivators' such as the work we are doing, the responsibility we have, and the recognition we get. Basically we can be satisfied enough to go to work but it takes something more to make us productive when we get there.

In practical terms this means that the things that make us want to go to work are not necessarily the things that motivate us to work more enthusiastically. Think about and answer these three questions:

1. What makes you go to work?
2. What makes you work when you get to work?
3. What makes you do a little extra?

If you find that the things that motivate you are the challenge or being given responsibility and authority then ask yourself whether with your own staff you can come up with the same kind of motivators.

Abraham Maslow's hierarchy of needs

Abraham Maslow produced a hierarchy or 'staircase' of needs. He said that the human moves up this hierarchy. As the lower-level needs are satisfied, then we aspire to the higher-level needs. The hierarchy can be represented by the staircase shown in Figure 1.1.

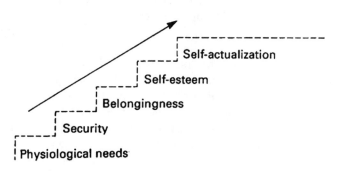

Figure 1.1 *Maslow's Hierarchy of Needs*

There are theorists who do not accept all of this hierarchy and there are some who have come up with their own. However, Maslow's is the best known, and it adequately represents the main point of agreement that higher-level needs such as 'self-actualization' (reaching potential, making decisions and taking risks, accepting and using authority and responsibility) can only come into effect after lower-order needs have been met. That is, unless our basic needs for security and health requirements are met then we will not be able to aspire to higher needs.

There are a number of theorists who have produced models of what motivates us. I have mentioned three of them to give a flavour of the concern which is shown to understand how we are motivated at work. This helps in the design, or redesign, of work to ensure more motivated and therefore more productive workers. It also assists in the training of managers and trainers, in that if we can understand the needs of individuals and groups, we can therefore help managers and trainers to meet those needs.

But how, in practice, does motivational theory apply to the design of induction? The following case study of Martin illustrates some of the points I have made.

Martin's experience

Martin was a manager in a large national organization. Married, with two very young children, he had worked for the organization for about six years in the north of England. After this time he was offered and accepted a transfer to Edinburgh, basically because his wife had never been particularly happy in the area in which they had been living.

Martin immediately ran into a series of problems because of the transfer. They made the mistake of not understanding the English legal system too well. On the basis of an agreement to sell their house, they bought one in Edinburgh. When the sale in England fell through they found themselves paying the equivalent of two mortgages. Although a certain amount was paid by the organization in respect of the transfer, it in no way covered the shortfall.

Also, because of the difficulty in selling the house and the need for it to be occupied in order to show it to its best advantage, Martin was living on his own for several months in a bedsit in Edinburgh while his family remained in the north of England.

Additionally, not long after the move, his department was involved in a major change within the organization due to new Government legislation. Martin was requested to take a major role in this. He was delighted at the recognition it gave him. Unfortunately, he simply could not cope with the number of stress factors inherent in all the changes he was experiencing. Because he was living away from his family, and under the threat of financial ruin, he was deprived of basic security and necessary relationships. Therefore he could not satisfactorily carry out the work expected of him to the best of his ability. This in turn increased the strain on him.

Although Martin's problems were finally resolved, he was left with the impression that during all his time under pressure, his worries were not adequately recognized by managers or those people in the organization best placed to help him. He should not have been given such an important job when he was under so much personal pressure, and his manager should have been aware of his predicament and assisted him through it. I shall discuss in Chapter 8 how the manager could have ensured a more supportive role.

Introducing Training and Development

Training and development of staff is, or should be, an integral part of the operation of any successful organization. Therefore we should be concerned that all staff are committed to any training which is on offer. Many of us have experienced poor trainers and the experiences usually colour our impressions of the organizations carrying out the training. If we were in the position of buying in the training we would not use trainers who were not effective. If we are dissatisfied with any course or programme laid on by our organization it will influence our attitude to all training staff, to the training unit or to training in general.

Therefore if you want new staff to be keen on training and development right from the beginning, then you have to make sure that that training is carried out properly from the beginning. Therefore, new staff and trainees should be impressed with the content of their first training experience in your organization. That is their induction programme. They should be impressed by trainers and they should look forward to further training. Therefore induction programmes should really be staffed by those trainers who:

- Are most able to design relevant, quality training.
- Are most likely to commit and motivate.
- Are able to help participants enjoy training courses.
- Are competent and experienced trainers.

A Catalyst for Organizational Change

If any organization is concerned to respond positively to the culture outside the organization – that is, if it wants to know what is going on in other organizations – it has to carry out research. This research may take different forms, from market research to find out what the customer wants, to an examination of school-leaver trends in order to plan future intake.

One method of researching and responding to change is to take into consideration the views, experience and attitudes of people new to the organization. New employees come with views of the organization from the outside. They come with fresh ideas, possibly hoping to have a role in influencing their new organization based on how they have seen it.

If the role of induction is simply to acclimatize new entrants and get them used to the new organization, then that organization is doing itself a disservice in the long term. Induction should be a two-way process, ensuring that the views, aspirations and concerns of all new employees are a factor in decision-making about organizational change if it is required. We may only know if it is required if we do the research.

Several years ago I was responsible for running induction courses for large groups of new entrants into a large national organization. The organization was an old-fashioned, bureaucratic affair, responding unwillingly to imposed changes from a central directorate rather than actively forecasting the factors they would have to respond to in the future. Unfortunately for the organization, at that time 95 per cent of the entrants were bright, capable and qualified school-leavers with high expectations of working life. They may have expected democracy and an independent way of working, with authority and responsibility. They certainly expected new technology, promotion and good training.

Unfortunately, the organization was unable to fulfil these expectations. The organization had resisted new technology like the plague. It had an autocratic and disciplinarian management-style, and the promotion prospects were few and far between and based on time-serving rather than on ability.

In short, the organization was taking on eager young new staff under false pretences. And, just as bad, it completely ignored the message coming through about the expectations of these young people. It should have been apparent that if these new staff were to be kept then the organization would have to recognize them and adapt to them.

Induction in a Changing Environment

At any ordinary time it is important that those entering an organization or taking up new posts or new work are properly introduced to their new work, environment and colleagues.

We live in an ever-changing economic and technological environment in which it is sometimes difficult for existing staff to come to terms with change, let alone staff who are being introduced to an organization for the first time. Some organizations have been experiencing more dramatic change than others. Hospitals and other health services have seen the change from national to local management involving such issues as local pay bargaining. Medical practices have become 'fund holders'. Water and electricity boards have become privatized as have many other services. Local authorities are undergoing major reorganizations and many local authority and central government functions are being contracted out to the private sector.

Because of the scale of change it is even more important that new staff entering an organization are aware of the history, the present status and the future developments within the industry and within the organization. Induction within such major change may not necessarily differ very much from standard programmes but it is essential that the content of the programme is up to date, and delivered by staff who are up to date, if new staff are not to feel that they are entering a confused, disgruntled or insecure organization.

One local authority presently faced with amalgamation with another is running two-day courses called 'Taking Stock'. These are to allow staff to consider their strengths and weaknesses in the light of forthcoming changes so they can take advantage of the changes while ensuring that they are not frightened by them. Another major organization faced with similar changes has implemented a series of courses for their training officers called 'Induction in a Changing Environment'. This is designed to help staff implement 'rolling' induction programmes that address change in the industry.

Effects of Induction on Existing Staff

There is evidence that providing induction for new staff can have a positive effect on present staff. This can happen in a number of ways. First, as discussed in the section above, we can learn about our competitors through information which new staff bring with them. For instance, technical staff may realize that they are less advanced than they thought they were when they talk to staff who have arrived from competitors or from overseas. This can have the effect of making them want to update their knowledge.

When staff are asked to design induction training it can have the effect of making them more aware of their own organizations. If they are preparing materials it usually means analysing the organization in order to get a complete overview. They may also be asked questions by new staff which they cannot answer. This means that they have to find out the answers.

By getting less motivated staff involved in inducting new recruits we can sometimes improve their motivation by giving them the extra responsibility for new staff. This should be done with caution, however, as a demotivated staff member may also demotivate the recruit.

Contribution to quality

Chapter 9 examines the emergence of issues relating to quality, particularly those of working to the standards attached to such initiatives as Investors in People and BS5750/ISO9000. The Investors In People initiative requires staff to be properly inducted and that this induction be evaluated. This contributes to the overall quality of training and development. BS5750/ISO9000 and Total Quality Management (TQM) are quality initiatives built on systems to which all staff should adhere. There is a requirement for adequate training in such systems and it is sometimes forgotten that this should start with systematic induction.

▶ ACTIVITY ◀

Consider the turnover in your own organization over the past year. Write down the benefits to you, to your department or to your organization if this turnover had been half of what it was.

2 Who Should Receive Induction Training?

▷   CHAPTER SUMMARY   ◁

- Induction training is a necessity for those who are joining new organizations or embarking on new careers.
- Induction programmes should be based on individual needs but we should consider the needs of particular groups.
- Induction training is also important for people taking on new jobs within an organization or when new developments are introduced. It is also important for people returning to work after long illnesses.
- It is also important that staff about to take up work abroad are fully inducted.
- The importance of inducting visitors and contractors is becoming increasingly recognized as is the importance of proper briefing of new and existing staff starting National or Scottish Vocational Qualifications.

The answer to the question in the chapter title is that induction is for anyone who is joining a new organization, moving from one part of an organization to another, taking up a new post or working with new people, or possibly working abroad.

Induction is often concerned with people starting work for the first time, whereas it has wider significance if we consider all the new things we do. Here is a sample:

start school   join a youth club or organization

start college or university	join a professional institute
go abroad	join a parent – teachers'
start work	association
join a social club	retire

In fact, induction is something that should happen to us time and time again. Sometimes it is not a major requirement if an organization is small or we only have a peripheral interest. Sometimes, however, the lack of induction to an organization can have a significant influence on whether we remain with it. If you think back to groups, clubs or educational courses you joined, you can easily remember dissatisfaction of some nature. It might have been the fact that no introductions were made and you felt isolated and uncertain. Perhaps the objectives of a course were not made clear and you were not sure what you were expected to do. Possibly you were not sure who was responsible for what, when and how.

Induction does have major importance when we are embarking on a new career, changing career or starting a training or educational course. It is at the beginning of these that we have to be sure that induction is thorough and professional for all who are starting out or changing direction.

But to what extent does it apply to everyone? In Chapter 4 we look at how the content of an induction programme depends on the things an entrant *must*, *should* and *could* know. I shall explain there that induction must be based on what any individual requires to know or be aware of in order to be satisfactorily inducted into the organization.

Different Categories of Newcomers

Having said that induction should be based on an analysis of individual needs, we nevertheless have to consider general categories of newcomers and their particular needs. See, for example, the list below. Can you add to it?

Women returners	Redundant managers
Long-term unemployed	Physically disabled
Ethnic groups	School-leavers
Older workers	Ex-offenders
Ex-Service personnel	Graduates

Although it might be considered odious to put people into pigeonholes, it is nevertheless necessary to consider particular difficulties faced by particular groups so that these difficulties can be eliminated or lessened and quicker integration be made possible. Training staff and managers must also have some way of preparing themselves for these categories of entrants if they are to work successfully at retaining them. We shall look at this later when we consider induction as part of a system. Let us look for the moment at particular needs and how they can be met.

Women Returners

When women return to work they very often do so with difficulty, having had to make arrangements for child-minding or other domestic matters. When others return to work or move job there is certainly a lot of stress and sometimes worry. With women returners this stress can be added to by worrying about what is happening at home. This worry can easily cause lack of attention and can so easily be misinterpreted as lack of interest.

Therefore it is absolutely essential that there is enough flexibility and consideration at the beginning of a job or training or educational course to allow for any settling-in periods due to changes in domestic circumstances. We should also be sure that women returners are aware of any provisions for staff welfare that could assist them in times of difficulty. More than this, those organizations that in the future make provision for child care, nurseries or after-school care will be in a better position to attract and retain a wider choice of candidate offered by the inclusion of women returners.

In order to attract women returners there are now companies that have decided to gear their production to the availability of female employees, by adopting flexible working rather than ask employees to fit into rigid shift patterns. Such flexible working includes:

flexible working round school hours	home working
term-time working only	job-sharing
teleworking	

It is interesting to note that one organization offering such flexible working to existing staff found as many men as women applying. Teleworking, mentioned above, is the use of technology to utilize the skills of people working from home or in rural 'telecottages', ie centres where local businesses and other organizations can use the available technology such as access to the Internet and desktop publishing.

One publishing organization is using the skills of around 20, mostly women, working on a part-time basis from home in remote rural areas. These women had already been trained in teleworking skills but to meet the need for induction and personal support, the organization has

31

employed a full-time manager who is in direct touch with these staff using electronic communications as well as travelling round as required.

Sometimes induction and other training courses are carried out in locations away from the normal place of work. In my experience this often causes female staff more difficulty with domestic arrangements than it does males. Because of difficulties in arranging care for children, or because of chauvinist attitudes of partners, it has simply not been possible for a woman to go away for training. Therefore thought should be given to contingency plans for such occasions. These could possibly involve:

Visits by travelling training staff.
Locally devised induction courses by trained managers.
Open learning.
Induction booklets.

last In common with the long-term unemployed, women returners to employment may be discouraged by a low sense of self-worth, a lack of confidence and a self-perceived lack of skills. Therefore, trainers must be able to build into induction programmes exercises or other methods to help women recognize their skills and abilities. This is usually best done alongside similar new entrants. As part of an induction programme for women returners or others, courses in personal development and assertiveness can be a successful way of helping new entrants cope with the challenges and demands, not just of work or training, but of their changed domestic circumstances.

Long-term Unemployed

Similar conditions apply to the unemployed and to the long-term unemployed in particular. Although we cannot expect every trainer or manager involved in induction programmes to have been unemployed themselves, we can at least expect them to have some empathy with those who have been unemployed for a long time. It is very difficult, especially for young people who have never been unemployed, to consider the plight of, say, a 35- to 40-year-old married man with a family, who has been out of work for two years. But this is sometimes what faces young and inexperienced staff in the Benefits Agency or on government training schemes.

Trainers or others meeting the unemployed should try to consider the frustrations, prejudices and attitudes towards government or anyone else whom they might perceive as having caused their unemployment. Very often, long-term unemployed people feel neglected and left out of society. These people may be resentful of government officials and trainers on government training programmes. Therefore it is vitally important that trainers are able to establish relationships with such entrants at an early stage. This can only come about if trainers understand the needs and the problems of the long-term unemployed and are willing to work with them and relate to them. Therefore, the question is whether the staff involved in induction programmes have the necessary skills to encourage, motivate and work with the unemployed.

Ethnic Groups

Clearly, if an organization is going to be committed to employing those from other ethnic backgrounds then they have to be sure that staff who recruit and induct are totally committed to policies of equal opportunity and that these policies are seen to be carried out in a positive way. The following checklist may help us determine whether our staff are fully following a positive policy:

- Are we fully equipped to deal with any language barriers by having access to interpreters as necessary?
- Are our trainers and supervisors trained to relate to these people by understanding their social background and conditions?
- Do we know about the educational and qualifications systems if we are dealing with immigrants or refugees?
- Do we have access to referral agencies which can give us advice?
- Are our training materials adaptable to different languages and cultures?
- Do we have an equal opportunities policy and are all our staff both aware of it and committed to it?

Older Workers

As with other categories of new workers, older workers bring with them special factors for consideration. They may have been out of the job market for several years or be transferring from one job to another.

When inducting mature workers we have to be sure that our trainers and supervisors understand that this group of people may not necessarily be returning to work just for the money but also for the interest and companionship in working with others of a like mind.

Financial changes may have made it more of an incentive for these people to work and they may well be shopping around for the best deal. To attract them, organizations will have to be prepared to produce the sort of package which will offer flexibility, and this may include optional part-time working.

We may also have to respect the fact that mature workers have come from a variety of backgrounds and may have held down quite high positions. I know of one senior Civil Servant who took early retirement and is packing engineering components in Edinburgh. Therefore we have to be prepared to accept and respect the maturity and often the experience they bring with them, even if they are being recruited for routine tasks. Many older staff will simply not tolerate being abused by supervisors or others who do not treat them with respect.

Ex-Service Personnel

Many ex-service personnel are to be found working in security organizations or as janitors for education departments and housing organizations. It is not generally known that most ex-service personnel go through de-briefing training and have access to many educational and training opportunities to help them prepare for the world beyond the services. In fact, they may have good qualifications and training, depending on their length of service, as the Forces in many cases provide highly specialized training and experience which should be taken into account and not dismissed as irrelevant. One of the quickest ways to demotivate is not to recognize previous learning, or worse, to denigrate it by making ill-advised and uninformed comment about it.

Redundant Managers, Executives, Business People

People in this group also have their own special needs. Again it is a question of trying to find out some background to the individuals coming into our organization. We might find that because of personal failure in business or because of redundancy, these people have low self-esteem and a feeling of personal failure and rejection. The fact that they are no longer bosses and in control may make them more reluctant to accept direction or orders from others. We may also have to consider during the induction period whether these entrants have financial or domestic problems generated by business failure or unemployment.

Whether or not their businesses have failed, or managers have been made redundant, we also have to consider the fact that they bring with them a wealth of valuable experience from the businesses in which they were involved. It is essential that trainers know about this and take it into account when designing induction programmes.

Physically Disabled and those with Medical Problems

We must also consider the special needs of a wide range of those who are disabled or who have medical complaints. I have experienced several cases of young people who were afraid to tell new employers that they suffered from diabetes, epilepsy or other conditions they found embarrassing. The consequences of not explaining the problem could be potentially dangerous, and employers should make it clear that they are approachable about such matters and will be sympathetic and discreet.

We should realize that there are few people who do not have some particular need which can be catered for sympathetically if we know in advance about it. Sometimes needs are so obvious that it has been an embarrassment to trainers or supervisors who have not been told in advance and who could otherwise have prepared.

The Government, through the Employment Department, publishes a range of booklets, newspapers and videos aimed at those who recruit and manage disabled people. These publications show that the employment of disabled workers need not be difficult. Those involved in designing induction programmes should be aware of these publications (see the Select Bibliography). One of the publications referred to is the *Code of Practice on the Employment of Disabled People*. This is published by the Employment Service. Their advice to those involved in inducting new staff who are disabled is:

In addition to normal induction for all employees, you may need to consider whether a new employee with a disability, or an employee who has become disabled, has any special needs in order to settle smoothly into a job. Discuss such needs with the worker concerned and the appropriate manager or supervisor. Examples would be:

- Assistance for people with limited mobility, such as parking facilities close to the workplace or slightly staggered starting and finishing times to avoid any crush;
- Taking early steps to help blind employees become familiar with the layout of their workplace;
- People who need to take medication being given an opportunity to do so in privacy;
- People who may occasionally need to stand or to sit being allowed to do so.

    –   Where a blind person has a guide dog, providing some-
where for it to be kept.

As with other employees, you should also make sure that people with
disabilities know who to approach if they have any particular
difficulties.

School-leavers

Earlier in this book I described an organization which did not keep
itself up-to-date with the hopes and aspirations of young school-leavers
they were taking on. The young people were joining because they had
high hopes of good career prospects and interesting work in a high-
tech environment. In fact what they were met with was a Victorian
culture dominated by authoritarian managers. The work was mundane
and routine and the career prospects were poor. The new entrants
soon came to have little respect for management and the turnover rate
became a problem.

We have to recognize in our induction programmes that school-
leavers are individuals and credit them with different levels of ability,
maturity, awareness and a range of attitudes. Therefore, the more individualized an induction programme, the more credibility it will have
with each and every new entrant to an organization.

Constructing an individual programme with each new entrant will
necessarily involve the young person spending time with someone
responsible for its design and implementation. If the right person is
chosen to do this and the induction programme is right for the individual then there is more chance that the young entrant will stay. If each
school-leaver is dealt with as an individual but allowed to be with others
during common elements of the programme, then there will be more
chance of a lower turnover rate, as we are recognizing individuality but
allowing interaction with those with the same worries and concerns on
joining a new organization.

As a school-leaver, my first job was in engineering. My memories
were that the organization, who were employing ten other apprentice
technicians, carried out an excellent induction programme making use
of many of the things advocated in this book including:

- A full week of induction training.
- Induction to off-the-job training (college).
- An appointed supervisor.
- Rotation through a number of departments for familiarization.
- A log book checked by the appointed supervisor.

- A residential training week designed to develop personal effectiveness, teamwork and belongingness.

In short, the above was a well-organized programme over the first year. The way in which it was run, although not perfect, left a mark on me and subsequently has influenced my views on inducting young people.

However, although I believed that that induction programme was very good, I decided to accept a similar job in another engineering company because it was nearer my home and was better paid. Induction in this company was a complete contrast. On reporting on the first day I was told to go to the training school. There was obviously a mistake as they had been told that I was a first-year apprentice and were about to start me on basic training. As the senior training officer was on holiday I was left to roam about the factory for a week until the training officer turned up. Additionally, no one told me where I could eat or gave me any other information other than an Official Secrets Act document, which I was asked to sign without any explanation.

Thinking back, there were a lot of questions I could have asked at the interview to satisfy myself that the move was the right one. However, being young and inexperienced, I did not know the right questions to ask and wrongly assumed that the working conditions would be no less acceptable than in my previous employment. I had come from a culture in which it was second nature for the organization to communicate properly with new staff and, being fairly new to working life, I wrongly expected that that was the norm. Naturally the first days of that employment coloured my impressions and I firmly believe that it had a lot to do with my leaving there within the following year.

EXAMPLE OF GOOD PRACTICE

In one area in England, an Education Business Partnership (EBP) has set up a system whereby school-leavers who are interested in a particular career can, through work experience, 'shadow' a member of staff to give them a greater insight into that company. This allows them to determine whether or not they still want to join that company and also allows the company to sell themselves to the school-leaver. It also means that when the young person joins the organization, they will be more committed and the induction period will be shorter. As a by-product, it helps the organization's image.

Ex-offenders

When ex-offenders are entering employment we must be particularly careful that we treat their backgrounds in confidence unless they themselves wish to disclose information. The training of ex-offenders does imply that trainers are open-minded and accept that such offenders have as much right to employment, education and training as anyone else.

It is also important to remember that, like those leaving the Services, those who have been in custody may already have, or have acquired while in prison, new skills and learning that should be taken into account in the new employment or training.

Graduates

Similarly to school-leavers, graduates may have little experience of working life. However, they will have had some experience of life and of freedom: freedom of choice and freedom of thought. They will have qualifications and may be extremely confident, if not over-confident. They will be looking for the best use to be made of their learning and it may come as a shock to them to find that their university or college learning has often been an entrance requirement and the learning has to start all over again.

Professionals such as doctors, lawyers, accountants and engineers often start their careers with very little training in the other essential skills required in their occupations: that is, the skills for working with people, the skills for managing people and the skills for managing themselves within their new working environment. For this reason, professionals, as with others starting a new job or career, should, as part of their induction package, have a written training programme which will, over a manageable time, give them the skills to work with and manage others. In Chapter 3 there is a sample of such a training programme.

EXAMPLE OF GOOD PRACTICE

One large development agency based in Scotland has set up a mentoring service for new graduates who are not only embarking on a new career but are also undertaking an MBA programme. The organization recognizes the level of support which this requires. The 'mentors' are experienced administrators from a department different from the new staff member. The mentors are volunteers who mainly keep in touch and assist in any difficulties, whether with the course or with work. This scheme has been so succesful that there are plans to extend it to other new entrants.

Working abroad

In Chapter 1, I discussed the story of Simon who had difficulties when he had been sent abroad by his company to work. He had not been prepared for the new physical environment and this had a potentially dangerous outcome.

Whether or not staff are new to the organization, there is a major need to induct them if they will be working abroad, particularly for the first time. One major British company in the power equipment field occasionally has to recruit staff quickly and send them abroad, sometimes to inhospitable climates. They have taken the decision to produce a series of workbooks and videos introducing these new staff to the conditions, problems and issues when they are moving to those areas.

There are a number of important issues, such as the culture and the way business is done which can be very different from how things are conducted in Great Britain. Such issues, which may be included in an induction course, programme or pack are:

Travel: how is travel to be arranged to the country and what are the travel arrangements within the country? What are passport and visa requirements?

Currency: what are the currency, exchange rates, and banking arrangements including the use of credit cards?

Salary: how will salary be paid and what are the implications for the payment of tax and National Insurance in Great Britain?

Language: what is the language and are there dialects? Does language training have to be undertaken?

Culture: what are the main areas of cultural difference? How is business done? What protocols have to be observed in business and private life, including dress and behaviour?

Security: what are the security arrangements for staff travelling abroad? How can they quickly get help from police, embassies or consulates?

Health: what are the arrangements for medical insurance and treatment?

Family: if the family is moving, what are the implications for schooling and care? If not, how can contact be maintained and will trips home be paid?

Recreation: what are the recreational facilities? These may include such areas as further education.

Environment: what are the conditions like in that country? What temperatures can be expected and how should staff dress?

These are only a few of the many issues that confront staff moving abroad. It would be impossible to identify them all here. What would be required would be an analysis carried out using the knowledge of people from, or who have visited, the countries in question. For organizations sending staff to different countries there may be some common core issues, supplemented by country-specific issues.

It should also be remembered that even within Great Britain there can be dramatic climatic, cultural and political differences. There are significant differences between the south-east of England, the northern islands of Scotland and Northern Ireland. Staff moving within the British Isles should also be aware of any significant contemporary issues. The general point is that those inducting new staff should appreciate such differences and make sure that they are taken into account in induction.

Contractors and Visitors

It is being increasingly realized that there is a need to induct visitors and contractors, particularly where there are security or health, safety and hygiene considerations. In the nuclear industry, for example, there are well-established procedures both for the vetting and inducting of contractors and business visitors. This also applies to tourists and others going to visitor centres at nuclear power stations.

The very real security implications are evident here, as are the safety risks for uncontrolled visitors to large-scale sites such as are found in the construction, chemical, steel and metal industries. British Alcan Highland Smelters has two levels of induction, one of which is a presentation to contractors along with a *Contractor's Handbook*, which lays out the terms and conditions as well as the health, safety and security considerations. For first-time visitors such as consultants and company representatives there is a short safety presentation using an overhead projector. This covers the following:

General points
    register at time office
    fire alarm
    bottles, cans, gas lighters banned from site
    first-aid emergency services on site

Operational areas
    accompanied by guide
    wear appropriate personal protective equipment

stay close to guide
do not touch equipment or levers etc.
do not touch metal: aluminium looks the same hot or cold
beware of movement of vehicles and overhead cranes
no watches, credit cards, pacemakers or cameras

HAVE A SAFE AND ENJOYABLE VISIT

Another growing issue is in hygiene in the food industry, along with the security of the product. It has been quite clear in recent years how household names in the food and drink industry are vulnerable when foreign bodies are found in food or drink or they are found to be contaminated by bacteria. Whole sections of a community can be affected when the local food canning factory has produced contaminated food and production is stopped. The long-term effects of this can be immeasurable. This is why food and similar organizations are taking steps to protect the product. In some cases, particularly where there are visitor centres, these visitors are completely separated from production by screens and walkways. In one major seafood processing factory each visitor is asked to read, sign and comply with a set of rules to ensure the company complies with the Food Hygiene regulations.

It is quite clear that such organizations which take induction of visitors and contractors as seriously as the induction of staff are ensuring there is less of a health and safety risk to all, as well as protecting premises, equipment and their product. Such actions also assist with the general move towards quality as described in Chapter 9.

Staff Starting NVQ/SVQS

In Chapter 9 I discuss the growth of the new competence-based qualifications that are designed to be assessed in the workplace. Experience has shown that if these new qualifications are not introduced systematically to all who may have an involvement, then they are less likely to be successful. Any induction to the new awards should follow the same principles as an induction course for people starting a new job.

Experience has also shown that this introduction should be on two levels: a general introduction for all staff who may be interested, and a more detailed introduction to all those who show a specific interest. The general introduction may look like this:

Introduction by senior manager
Background to national standards
National Vocational Qualifications

NVQs in the .... industry
How you are assessed for the awards
Who will assess you
Timescale and support from assessors.

The more specific session would expand on the above, with potential candidates being given a chance to see an assessment take place, possibly on video.

NVQs/SVQs are revolutionizing the way in which skills and knowledge are acquired and recognized, and it is essential that they are introduced through systematic implementation planning, including proper induction.

Staff returning from illness

Staff returning to work after prolonged illness or other leaves of absence may be just as much in need of induction as newer members of staff. Depending on the illness, there may be a need for the support that can be provided through counselling or mentoring as part of the 're-induction' programme. This will be particularly true in organizations which are in the process of change and in which the absent member of staff finds that his or her job has changed, even in a small way.

With such members of staff it would be advisable to assist their re-introduction to the organization in much the same way as a new member of staff, but ensuring that only those areas of change are addressed. We have to remember that the member of staff may see themselves as an integral part of the organization and may not take kindly to a re-introduction session.

Fundamental to such a re-introduction would be examining the previous training and development plan to ensure that any discontinued activities are restarted if appropriate, and deciding whether the changes which have occurred in the organization will mean a new plan, which would also take into account any personal development undertaken during the absence.

EXAMPLE OF GOOD PRACTICE

The following is a document given to visitors to a large seafood processing factory.

VISITORS TO ...... PLANT

To be read by all visitors to the ...... plant.

This is a food manufacturing site and as such all employees and visitors have a duty to assure our customers that we achieve the highest standards of hygiene and food safety.

In order to do this we must avoid, knowingly, bringing food poisoning bacteria into the factory. The most likely sources of these bacteria are from 'tummy bugs' which cause severe sickness and/or diarrhoea, and also from infections of wounds, boils, throat and nose.

Should you, as a visitor to this site, be suffering or have recently suffered from any of the conditions listed or another infectious illness, please contact the senior manager via reception:

> Typhoid fever, cholera, tuberculosis, typhus fever, paratyphoid, amoebic or bacillary dysentery, any salmonella infection, any staphylococcal infection, food poisoning or suspected food poisoning.

As a visitor to the ... plant you will appreciate that there are certain rules that we must ask you to observe:

1. You will remove all jewellery before commencing a tour of the factory.
2. No eating, drinking or smoking is permitted outwith the canteen area.
3. Protective clothing is to be worn at all times inside the factory. This will be provided by your host, who will instruct you on its use.
4. All protective clothing is to be removed and disposed of after the factory visit.
5. Hands must be washed on initially entering the factory and again on moving from separate production areas. Sanitizer sprays must be used as directed.
6. Any other requests made during your visit, relating to food hygiene and food safety, must be followed.

SIGNING THE VISITORS BOOK INDICATES COMPLIANCE WITH THE ABOVE.

Job Handovers

Although induction is normally associated with staff joining an organization it is no less important for staff taking over a job from a current post-holder. On many occasions staff are expected to take over duties when the person doing them vacates the post through retirement, promotion, transfer or other reasons.

Some of us can remember times when we were asked to take over someone's job in such an event and also when it was difficult to fathom out how a job was to be done. We can remember the amount of time wasted in trying to figure out how the job which was done yesterday is to be done today.

Sometimes too we consider ourselves to be indispensable and do not make preparations for successors. Such succession planning is both good management and courtesy towards colleagues who have to step in if you are absent or have to leave for any reason.

With manual and technical skills it is less important to leave full details. For instance, a turner or welder could easily take over from another if details of the job are available. However, the more detailed and complicated the job the more time has to be taken in getting on top of it. It is particularly important in administrative posts.

Handover checklists

This is where handover checklists and job manuals are invaluable. Handover checklists are basically lists of the duties to be done and when they are to be done. They can also act as an everyday reminder and an aid to effective time management. An example is shown in Table 2.1.

Table 2.1 *Example of a handover checklist*

DUTY	WHEN	COMMENT
Check all staff in attendance.	9am each day	Absence details in file.
Staff meeting	10.30 Monday	Agenda on desk. Minutes in file
Sales staff meeting	Tuesdays, time variable	Chief exec. will brief by phone Tuesday am
Check stock levels in main stores	Wednesdays	Computer file 'Stock', see disk file
Order admin. stock	Thursday	Requisitions in drawer
Allocation of staff to duties for next week	Friday am	Duty sheets in file

This is a short sample of what is possible. An induction checklist can be as detailed as required. The amount of detail would probably be dictated by the complexity of the duties and the extent to which they are variable. It would be impractical to spend a disproportionate amount of time on such checklists but they are nevertheless a contribution to good planning.

Another contribution to good planning is the procedures manual, which is basically a collection on paper of all jobs which are done in a department or organization. These are constructed through the process of task analysis, which is anyway the basis of the design of training programmes. Task analysis starts by looking at every job which is done and then breaking them down to component parts or tasks. We then take the individual tasks and examine what is involved in them, as in the example in Table 2.2.

Table 2.2 *Example of a task analysis*

Job: Visitor Centre Escort

TASK	PROCEDURE/KEY POINTS

Greet visitors at reception	Get signature in visitor book
	Issue centre leaflets in appropriate language
	Guide to waiting area or shop; Tell when tour will start
	When 10–15 in group start tour
	Ensure audio-visual show ready:
	   – slides at beginning
	   – tape at beginning
	   – cinema clear and clean

Introduce tour	Refer to brief for talk Point out toilets
Start audio-visual show	Dim lights Start tape and projector

Start tour	According to map and tour brief
	Essential:
	   – visitors to keep between lines
	   – keep to tour party

End tour	Take questions Thanks and point to shop

Again this is only a short sample to show how many procedures can be set down on paper. It is probable that someone who had done this job for some time would not see the point in having this, as they would be quite sure of themselves and their ability to do the job. It is nevertheless a valuable training aid for new staff or if someone else has to do the job in a hurry. Although this would appear to be a simple job, it is amazing how easily new staff, especially young people, can get flustered simply by trying to remember the sequence of events in a job.

If we use this system to examine every job we can very quickly construct a comprehensive manual to cover every aspect of the work of a department, organization or even an industry. Such analyses are invaluable not only for induction training programmes but for the design of training programmes in general.

The above method of analysis is also invaluable when introducing any amount of staff to new developments in an organization. For example, when it was introducing computerized systems for the first time, one large company issued such manuals and checklists to supplement training courses. Such an approach is common with the introduction of new technology but is less so with manual systems, where it can be every bit as useful.

▶ ## ACTIVITY ◀

Consider the new recruits to your organization over the past year. Thinking back, did any of them have any particular needs that were only apparent after the recruits were taken on? What were those needs and what steps could now be taken to meet the needs of such future recruits?

3 What Shape Should Induction Take?

▷ SUMMARY ◁

- Case studies show how induction programmes can be poorly planned and inefficient.
- A model induction programme shows the components that go to making up a comprehensive system of induction.
- An example of an individually designed induction programme is shown.

Case Studies of Poor Induction Programmes

Having decided that induction is not a course but a programme or system, we then have to ask what it would look like in practice. First we can look at one or two case studies to see how induction can go wrong. Perhaps you can identify what things could possibly have been improved in these cases.

The Local Authority

This local authority, one of the largest in Great Britain, has a wide involvement in: education, roads and transport, social work, water and sewerage, libraries, and a range of other functions.

Induction to the organization was provided through a one-day course held at a central location. The course excluded all teaching staff for whom separate arrangements were supposed to be made and all manual staff for whom formal induction was not available.

All levels of administrative and professional staff from office juniors to senior managers were expected to attend the course. To some who attended, this was not a problem but it created some embarrassment and at times resulted in poor participation.

The course was based on giving information and selling the authority and its services. Some senior staff, used to working in local authorities and possibly already living in the area, could not understand why they were expected to give up valuable working time while adapting to a new job in order to attend what they considered an irrelevance.

The course was based mainly on a succession of guest speakers who were competent in their own fields but who were poor communicators and very often ineffective and even boring.

Staff attending had very often been in post for several months before attending.

As the course was carried out at a central location it meant that staff, some of them with domestic commitments, were expected to stay overnight in the city where the course was held. This in effect meant that they were away from home and work for two days rather than one.

The course was not well respected and, in some cases, influenced the views which many staff had of the operation of the central training unit. The course was run on the basis that a senior manager felt that an induction course should be provided and therefore one was. Unfortunately little thought was put into it and it was designed around what it was thought new entrants wanted rather than what was actually required by way of acclimatization to the authority. As a result not only was the course not rated but it clearly affected the credibility of the rest of the training staff.

Originally resistant to changing the course, the manager in charge finally agreed to set up a study group to consider ways in which the programme could be made more effective. The group came up with the following recommendations:

1. An induction checklist for staff that outlined the important points which each new entrant should be aware of.
2. An authority directory outlining conditions of service. It was a strange thing that this had never existed.
3. The formal involvement of line managers in the induction process mainly through ensuring that induction checklists were completed.
4. Training of departmental representatives or guest speakers in effective presentation and training techniques.

Some of these will be discussed later, as they are all valid methods of improving induction.

The Civil Service Department

A large Civil Service department with a regional training base servicing 3,000 staff was responsible for running induction courses for all basic grade clerical staff. Higher grade staff had induction programmes drawn up on an individual basis. This induction course was combined with a customer relations course. As a course it was considered effective but the following gave rise to criticism:

1. Often staff would be in post for several months before being called to attend induction courses. If, during the first dates given, the entrant was absent or otherwise unavailable, then a further date would be given. On one occasion, one staff member who had been in post attended the induction course a full year after she started.

2. Problems were often experienced with young entrants away from home for the first time. Sometimes they would get into trouble through drinking too much or would disrupt proceedings in a number of ways.

3. There was an agreement with trade unions for a guest speaker to attend the induction course and brief the new entrants on involvement with trade unions. This was done without any training staff present and was often counter-productive to the philosophy of the course as it was based on one individual's perception of management and discouraged entrants who sometimes complained about what was being said. As it was a union agreement it was nevertheless kept in.

4. Courses were very often over-subscribed, with as many as twenty attending at times.

Although this course was generally effective it was probably more to do with the fact that it was linked to a course on customer relations, which was enjoyable and received good reports. The induction section was less than successful and merited change.

If we look at a model training programme we can see how some of the problems could be resolved. Figure 3.1 shows a possible plan for a programme.

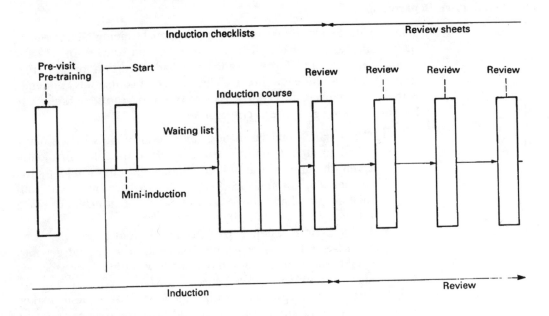

Figure 3.1 *A model induction programme (schematic)*

A Model Induction Programme

Having looked at a plan for a model induction training programme it is necessary to see what this would look like in practice when applied to the individual new entrant. In Table 3.1 there is an example of what an individually designed programme might look like on paper. This is followed by a detailed look at the components of an integrated induction programme.

Table 3.1 *A sample induction programme*

Name: David Alexander
Department: Research and Development
Start date: 2/7/19–
Line manager: Stephen Davies
Training Unit Contact: David Brodie

INDUCTION PROGRAMME

1. Pre-visit
  As David is new both to the job and to the area, the company has agreed,

as part of the relocation package, to fund a visit to the area and to the company before the official starting date. This visit will take place on 26 and 27/6/19–. The first day of the visit will be used by David and his wife Jane to look at prospective new houses. I have already arranged for the personnel department to send details from local estate agents.

On the second morning David will visit the company to clear up one or two pressing personnel and administrative problems. The following is the programme.

09.30 David will report to gatekeeper who will issue a temporary pass. Mary Christie at Personnel will be phoned and will meet David and escort him to the Personnel Department. David will be introduced to all appropriate staff and any administrative matters should be cleared up. It is important that all salary details are recorded and expense forms are issued.

10.30 Mary should escort David to his new department where he will be met by his manager, Stephen Davies. David should be introduced to his new colleagues and any worries he has cleared up.

2. *Initial Induction Course*

As a place on an appropriate induction course will not be immediately available, it is essential that an initial induction session be carried out on the first day. This should be based on the official induction guidelines for scientific staff. The following content is suggested:

Priority health and safety
    Point out emergency exits.   Issue protective clothing.
    Explain emergency drill.   Point out barrier cream and ear plugs.

    First-aid post and personnel.   Point out danger areas.
Domestic arrangements
    Explain flexible working system.   Toilets and rest room.
    Issue key.   Ensure desk and bench area now available.

    Factory tour.   Issue stores requisition and take to stores.

    Canteen.
Other
    Issue Official Secrets Act and get signature.

3. *Induction Course*

This will take place at the Central Training Unit on 13 and 14/8/–. The course will be composed almost entirely of new scientific staff, mainly graduates. Below is a summary course programme. A full course programme will be issued with the joining instructions:

Day 1
09.30 Welcome and introductions.
       Address by Chief Executive, Annette McDonald.
       Coffee and discussion.
10.15 The ... Scientific Company
       History   Markets

Structure	Competitors
Geography	Future Developments
Products	

11.30 The company and its commitment to the local environment and society.

12.30 Lunch in staff canteen.

14.00 Group tour of factory including short presentations by managers of:

Marketing	Company doctor/nurse
Personnel	Stores

16.00 Review of day and group discussion.

Day 2

09.30 Health and safety in the scientific environment.

11.30 Quality procedures:
   Introduction to quality system ISO9000.
   The use of the quality manual.
   Quality monitoring procedures.

12.30 Lunch in staff canteen with personnel and training manager.

13.30 Training and development.
   Further education scheme.

14.30 Security and the Official Secrets Act.

15.00 Final discussion and review.

4. *Individual Training Plan*
20/8/19– at 10.30 am has been provisionally set for this meeting with David Brodie of the training staff. The purpose is to determine what training and development will be required by David over the first year with the Company.

5. *Review of Induction Procedures.*
This first review will be carried out at a mutually agreed date in the first week of November. The purpose is primarily to ensure that David is settling in and nothing is getting in the way of his making progress.

The secondary, but important, reason is to ensure that all health and safety, administrative and personnel matters have been taken care of satisfactorily.

Induction will again be reviewed at the first staff appraisal which will be carried out in about six months' time.

The Pre-visit

Assuming that recruitment has been carried out, we now look at how we can make the best start to induction. Often new recruits put all their efforts into preparing for interview and presenting themselves in the best way possible. It is only after the decision to join a new organization has been made that all of the practical implications of a new job have to be faced. Obviously when considering a new position we do consider the priorities. But there are normally a hundred-and-one other things that a new recruit and his or her partner have to consider. This is particularly true if the job is in a new area and houses have to be bought and sold, children have to move school, and any number of practical problems have to be dealt with.

One way of addressing this problem is to offer, where required, a pre-visit to the area or to the organization. Some organizations do offer this and pay expenses for the trip as part of a relocation package. A relaxed visit to the organization to meet new superiors and staff informally before the starting date is a way to acclimatize the new starter more quickly by removing the often real worry of meeting new staff. It also allows for meeting personnel representatives to sort out any financial matters. On a more basic level it also helps the new entrant to see how people dress and where they eat so that he or she can be more prepared for the first day.

And not only does it assist senior staff to acclimatize. It can also be a very useful exercise for younger workers. One organization takes this a stage further and invites fairly large groups of potential staff in their last year at school to spend some time working in their factory, in the confidence that a number of the school-leavers will decide to apply for positions. Although this may be considered to be recruitment it is still a way to introduce local young people or others to the culture existing in the organization. Not only does this attract staff, it is also good public relations.

One training organization is even more advanced in offering to large local employers a pre-recruitment training scheme which is geared to the needs of that organization. This training is funded by a Training and Enterprise Council and has already demonstrated that informing prospective staff about the organization before recruitment improves retention rates.

Whether they be for one prospective member of staff or a dozen, pre-visits or pre-training help to cover a number of administrative issues, allowing new starts to get on with the job of becoming used to the organization. That entrant is even more likely to want to stay if he or she sees that the organization is concerned enough to invite a pre-visit.

The Mini-induction

One of the problems identified in our case studies above was the fact that in some instances staff had to wait several weeks or months before attending induction courses. Given that one of the reasons for having induction is establishing credibility for training in general, then it is hardly doing the job by asking staff to attend a course well after the time they really need it. One way of getting round this problem is having what could be called a 'mini-induction'. If we have a system in which staff have to wait a number of weeks for a full induction course because of high recruitment or other reasons, then mini-inductions can be arranged.

These mini-inductions should consist of priority information which the entrant needs to be aware of at the beginning of work. It should be done within the first couple of days and can be carried out by an immediate supervisor or delegated to a responsible and credible member of staff. A programme for a mini-induction might look like the example in Table 3.2.

Table 3.2 *An example of a mini-induction*

Jenny Smith
Trainee Systems Designer

INITIAL INDUCTION SESSION
Jenny will be reporting to work at 9.00 am and will be met by her immediate supervisor, Kay Wright.

Monday 5 May
9.00–10.00
Kay should spend the first hour simply introducing Jenny to the rest of the staff who should be briefed to explain their role in the department. Tell Jenny that she will receive a chart showing all members of staff and their functions.

10.00–10.20
Kay and one or two others should take Jenny to the staff tea-room and tell her about the tea fund and about lunch arrangements.

10.20–11.00
Kay or a delegated member of staff should take Jenny to Alan Archibald at Personnel who will be waiting for her.
   The following should be covered briefly:

1. Check salaries department has all relevant details required.
   – P45
   – Bank details
   – N.I. Number
2. Check Jenny knows how she is to be paid.
3. Ask whether an advance is required.
4. Give pensions etc. booklet but stress that the subject will be covered on the full induction course.
5. Issue expenses claim forms for relocation.

Introduce to all relevant staff in personnel.

11.00–13.00
Alan should take Jenny back to her department and hand her back to Kay. By this time Jenny's desk should be in place. Leave her some time to sort out her things then check that she is comfortable. Kay to delegate someone to take her to staff canteen or check out preference.

13.00–14.00
Lunch

14.00–16.30
Kay to outline departmental projects and introduce her to Tom Robertson with whom she will be working over the next few weeks.
Issue:
Departmental chart.
Company organizational chart.
Minutes of last three staff meetings.
Holiday rota and tell her about advance arrangements.
Administration manual.
Organizational telephone directory.

16.30–17.00
Kay to spend last half hour with Jenny checking whether there are any problems and checking whether she knows exactly what she will be doing over the next few weeks.

John Stevenson
Personnel and Training Manager

I would hope that in such an event many supervisors would organize such a first day. By putting it down on paper we formalize the system and ensure that nothing is omitted. Such a system, if all appropriate staff have copies of the programme, will help to instil a positive approach to dealing sensitively with staff on their first day.

The Letter of Invitation and the Waiting List

In my experience many people attending induction and other courses sometimes receive little or no notice about when they should attend. For mainly domestic arrangements it is important that participants receive adequate notice of attendance. This should be done formally by letter, preferably signed by the head of department or head of training. This letter formalizes the course and immediately sets a standard of administration for training that new entrants can look forward to. It also indicates to the new staff member that he or she can look forward to a professionally run course. A sample letter of invitation is shown in Table 3.3.

Table 3.3 *A sample letter of invitation*

Jenny Smith
Trainee Systems Designer
Computing Services Department

Dear Jenny,

Induction Course, 3 and 4 May 19–

I have pleasure in letting you know that a place has been reserved for you on the forthcoming Induction Course to be held in the Central Training Unit.

The course will be run by training officers Gerry Davidson and May Carson whom you can contact at the training centre before the course if you have any queries. Please also let them know if for any reason you cannot attend or if you have any special requirements.

Please bring with you the induction checklist you were issued on your first day.

I have enclosed a copy of the course programme.

I look forward to meeting you during the first session of the course.

John Stevenson
Personnel and Training Manager

If any waiting time is required, and the organization is large, resulting in there being a number of new entrants for a limited number of courses, then it is important that a waiting list is kept of those due to go on courses. When the waiting list reaches a predetermined number or maximum waiting time, then the waiting list would be deemed to be full and a new one started. At this point all new entrants would be sent a letter of invitation as above and arrangements for the course would be made.

The Induction Course

Although I have already said that induction is not a course but a system, the induction course can be an important part of that system for a number of reasons. When recruits start with a new organization they can be at a psychological disadvantage because of some of the reasons put forward in Chapter 1. That is, they may be worried, apprehensive and unsure of themselves in a new environment. Obviously with more experienced and senior staff this would be less of a problem if they are used to moving from one organization to another. Indeed some individuals and families in the Services or Civil Service take moving from place to place in their stride.

The induction course serves as a common starting point for all new entrants and allows individuals to form common bonds and share worries or concerns. It can be easier to talk to another person in the same boat than it would be to someone who has been in the organization for some time.

It can also be the start of team-building within the organization. It is generally recognized that people in organizations work better as a team and it is for this reason that many companies invest in team-building, particularly for managers. However, team-building is no less important for supervisors and all other staff. If they learn together and get to know one another then there is more chance that they will work together and not let one another down.

I remember two linked Government departments whose staff were constantly at loggerheads, with the result that the public suffered due to misinformation and lack of communication. It was decided to do some joint training, a result of which was less friction as each department began to understand the other's problems. Most of this understanding came simply from staff of each department meeting one another and realizing that they were all trying to do a similar job and had the same problems. It was all too easy to be angry with unknown faces. Team-building at an early stage, such as induction, would clearly have avoided many problems, including dissatisfaction by the public.

The induction course may also be the place to sell the organizational culture to the new entrant. Many organizations wish to maintain standards within their operations. These may be standards of behaviour and conduct within the factory or office. There may be standards of conduct towards customers or clients. There could be standards of timekeeping and dress which the organization would like to maintain. The induction course is one way of establishing standards by raising the issue and allowing new entrants to discuss them. Standards are more easily implemented if they are negotiated rather than imposed. As in a previous example, if an induction course is linked to another aspect such as teambuilding or customer care, then other aspects of standards or behaviour can be learned.

The induction course training plan

In Chapter 2 I said that the length of an induction course will depend on what an entrant *must*, *should* and *could* know. It will also be determined by how much the organization delegates induction to line management and uses other methods which we shall discuss later. It will also be determined by the amount of resources an organization is willing or able to devote to the acclimatization of new staff.

Having said this, it would still be useful to give a sample outline course plan for an induction course. This is shown in Appendix 1. In this programme I have outlined not only the topics but examples of the ways in which subjects can be handled in an interesting way. This plan is set out in a format which I believe should be adopted for every such short training course. This does not mean that every course should be run in a rigid fashion following every last direction. What it does is give a structure to a course which can be modified when felt necessary. If such a training plan is being delivered by a number of different training staff, possibly working in teams, then the plan can be negotiated, with the best methods discussed and incorporated, sometimes as options.

The Individual Training Programme

In Chapter 2 I said that, especially for graduates, there should be a training programme negotiated and established at the beginning of the induction period. Induction can be the beginning of an individual's training experience within the organization and it is important that it gets off to a good start.

An individual training programme is based on an analysis of training needs. When a new entrant joins the organization, the personnel section should have a good idea of the skills and knowledge which that entrant possesses. However, it is still necessary that the 'skills gaps' are identified and provision made for training to be provided.

The example in Table 3.4 shows how an individual training programme can be set down and agreed during induction training.

Table 3.4 *An example of an individual training programme*

Alex Johnson
Trainee Manager-Retail
Agreed Training Plan
5/6/19– to 27/1/19–

DATE	TRAINING
5/6/19–	As Alex is new to the organization he should undergo full induction training as per the training guide. This should take the form of initial induction on his first day. This should be conducted by the store manager or deputy.
25/6 to 26/6	This should be followed by a full induction course carried out at the central training unit. New trainee managers from other locations will also be attending. See attached list.
24/8 to 26/8	As the job will involve a great deal of contact with the public, there will be a course on Customer Care held at the training centre.

28/9	Alex will accompany the store manager to the annual trade exhibition in Birmingham.
17/10 to 22/10	By this time Alex will be beginning to manage staff and attendance at a Junior Management course will be necessary.
25/1 to 27/1	Internal budgetary control course to be held at the training centre.

Obviously the length and depth of the training plan will be determined by the training required and by the prior learning and experience of the entrant. However, there are few cases in which a structured training plan of the above nature would not be considered a necessity. A commitment to training by the production of such a plan can encourage and motivate new recruits, as they can see that the organization is taking their development seriously.

The Induction Checklist

As stated elsewhere, induction should not be delegated wholesale to training staff. Managers and supervisors have the primary responsibility of carrying out induction training. One way to ensure that managers or delegated staff carry out induction is to have induction checklists. These are really only lists of the important things which a new entrant should know about or be aware of. A sample induction checklist is shown in Table 3.5. This is based on the engineering factory discussed earlier.

Table 3.5 *A sample induction checklist*

INDUCTION CHECKLIST ITEM	INITIALS	DATE
Health and safety		
Health and safety course	....	....
Health and safety policy issued	....	....
Medical examination	....	....
Protective clothing issued	....	....
Emergency exits	....	....
Danger areas	....	....
Emergency procedures	....	....
Barrier cream/ear plug dispenser	....	....
First-aider/post shown	....	....
Financial	....	....
Meeting with Personnel	....	....

Pension position clarified ....
Booklet issued ....
Salary details covered ....
Expenses system covered ....
Expense forms issued ....

Organizational
Introductions to colleagues ....
Tour of factory ....
Organizational chart issued ....
Stores system explained ....
Stores requisitions issued ....
Quality manual and procedures ....
Security system explained ....
Security pass issued ....
Official Secrets Act explained and signed ....
Parking pass issued ....

Training and development
Presentation on system and possibilities ....
Booklet issued ....
Training needs meeting ....
Further education scheme ....

Staff issues
Staff appraisal system ....
Disciplinary system ....
Grievance procedures ....
Equal opportunities policy ....
Trade Union presentation ....
Trade Union leaflets issued ....

INDUCTION CHECKLIST	SIGNATURE	DATE
COMPLETED		
Entrant	....	....
Manager/Supervisor	....	....
Training contact	....	....

This checklist is a sample of what might be appropriate in this case and would be based on what was considered important in this particular occupation or organization.

The Review of Induction

In Chapter 5 review of induction is discussed more fully and described as part of a continuing system designed both to acclimatize entrants successfully and to monitor and decrease the turnover rate. A sample form of review is shown in Table 3.6. This is again related to the induction checklist above (Table 3.5).

Table 3.6 *A sample review of induction*

Staff Member: David Alexander
Date of Entry: 2/7/19–
Department: Research and Development
Line Manager: Stephen Davies
Training Unit
Contact: David Brodie

PURPOSES OF REVIEW
1. Primarily to ensure that the new member of staff is satisfactorily settling in to the new position and there are no barriers to progress.
2. To ensure that all items on the induction checklist have been covered.

Health and safety
Has there been a satisfactory introduction to all matters related to health and safety and has the checklist been completed?

Comment:

Financial
Is the new entrant completely happy with the financial arrangements and have there been any difficulties which have not yet been cleared up?

Comment:

Organizational
Are there any problems related to the organization, including difficulties in getting on with the job. What can be done about this?

Comment:

Training and development
Has the training and development system been explained?
    Has the entrant been given the opportunity to discuss training needs and has a programme been drawn up?
    Has the further education system been explained and has the entrant decided on any course?
    Have there been any difficulties in the entrant following any agreed training or educational programmes?

Comment:

Staff issues
Have there been any difficulties related to staff issues?
Has the staff representation, grievance and disciplinary system been adequately explained?

Comment:

REVIEW COMPLETED	SIGNATURE	DATE
Staff member	....	....
Reviewer	....	....

As seen in the earlier illustration of a model induction programme, reviews of induction can be carried out at appropriate times, possibly after two months, then again at four months. After this it would merge into an appraisal system if one exists within the organization.

The review would probably take the form of a shorter version of the induction checklist seen earlier. Table 3.6 shows an example of what it might look like on paper.

It can be seen that the success of this review would probably depend on the level of openness that could be achieved. This openness would probably only be achieved if the review was carried out by an independent reviewer such as a training officer responsible for the induction programme. It would also only be successful if the review was carried out sympathetically but also objectively, that is, bearing in mind that organizations cannot always change to suit the individual. Nevertheless it is essential to ensure that we at least show concern for the feelings and the problems of the newcomer.

EXAMPLE OF GOOD PRACTICE

As part of their move towards the Investors in People initiative, a heating supplies company with an unacceptable level of staff turnover has implemented a working party to investigate all forms of training. Part of their remit is to produce an induction training programme that motivates new staff and which is interesting. The working party includes members of staff at all levels as well as their representatives, a consultant and training staff. The programme is to be piloted before it is accepted.

▶ ### ACTIVITY ◀

Consider the parts of an induction system as outlined here. Write down the barriers to implementing such a system, even in a scaled-down version. How could you overcome these barriers?

4 Designing an Induction Training Programme?

	CHAPTER SUMMARY	

 CHAPTER SUMMARY

- The design of an induction training programme should be based on the 'must knows', 'should knows' and 'could knows' of a new job.
- There should be specific outcomes of the programme described in terms of aims and objectives.
- The design of an induction programme should be based on a range of methods that make it stimulating.
- Those involved in induction training should be aware of the relevant National Standards.

One traditional way of looking at the content of induction courses and programmes is to make a list of all those things which a new entrant should know about. This would then form the basis of an induction course. Later we shall be looking at the problems that arise when, for instance, junior staff appear on the same courses as senior staff and directors. In many cases, the information which comes over on an induction course is simply not appropriate to the new entrants on that course.

The question is whether a director or senior manager joining an organization requires the same information as say, a 17-year-old with no experience of working life. Of course not! What we have to do is consider the appropriateness of the content of the induction training programme.

'Must knows', 'Should Knows', and 'Could Knows'

One good way to do this is through another training exercise in identifying: 'must knows', 'should knows' and 'could knows'. That is, for every individual entering an organization we have to ask three questions.

What things must a new entrant know?

Obviously there are many personnel matters such as holidays, wages, salaries, etc, which all new entrants must know about. However, not all new entrants will require to know about them in the same detail. Wages may be more important to the young entrant than pension rights, whereas the company pension may have been one of the attractions for the older recruit.

Many organizations have a number of sections or departments. In some departments health and safety training may be more of a priority than in others. For instance, health and safety is just as important in an office environment as it is on the building site. However, it is more important and more urgent that new entrants to construction get in-depth training in health and safety appropriate to their workplace before they go on site. Although it is important in an office, it is not so immediate. There will still be things, however, which are a priority and which new entrants will have to know about for their safety, for example, the location of the fire exits.

With health and safety, as with other subjects, there are general issues that are applicable to all. However, when it comes to specifics like construction or catering then it is more appropriate if in-depth training is carried out for specific target groups.

In essence, what I am saying is that the 'musts' of an induction programme would vary according to the people coming into the organization. Therefore we must learn to treat them on an individual basis and design training courses and programmes accordingly.

What things should a new entrant know?

The same thing goes for 'should knows'. Should knows are essentially those things a new entrant ought to know in order to fit quickly into an organization. For example, on joining one organization when I had just left school, I was not told until it was too late that I would have to take my holiday allowance by a certain date or I would lose it. It wasn't a life or death issue but it was something I really should have known about.

What things could a new entrant know?

'Could knows' are more likely those things which may be of interest to the new entrant but are not essential to his or her well-being. For example it may not be appropriate for every new entrant to know about the history of the organization. On the other hand, knowledge about the organization and what it has achieved may make some people more committed, more loyal and more motivated.

When considering 'should knows' and 'could knows', trainers and supervisors must take into account the prior learning of new entrants. One local authority with which I was involved as a training officer delivered a standard induction programme which included an introduction to that particular geographic area. This reflected the number of newcomers to the area. However, irrespective of whether a member of staff was a newcomer to the area or not, they were expected to sit through a fairly lengthy presentation on the wonderful benefits of living in that area. In addition, they also had to sit through a presentation on the operation of local government even though it was highly likely that they had come from another local authority.

One Government department receiving transferred staff from a different section of that department expected those entrants to sit through lengthy briefings on staff terms and conditions, irrespective of the fact that they might have been in the service for several years.

Again, we come back to considering the individual entrant to the organization rather than assuming that all new entrants are going to be of equal experience and status. It is only when each individual at any level is considered as requiring appropriate and individual induction that the induction process will be effective and productive.

Aims and Objectives

If we don't know where we are going we will not know when we get there. What I mean is that our training has to have some direction. But what direction are we to go in if we don't have a target? In training terms these targets are usually called 'aims and objectives' or sometimes 'outcomes'.

Every training course that a trainer designs, or indeed every presentation which a trainer or manager gives, should have aims and objectives.

Aims

Aims are statements of the general intentions of any training course rather than specific outcomes. For instance an aim of a first-aid course could be to 'provide staff who can give emergency treatment competently'. I would suggest that for any induction programme or course the aim might be:

This induction programme is designed to inform the participant of everything required for him or her to accept and settle into the organization quickly.

It is also designed to build a firm commitment to the organization and ensure that everything is done to make the entrant want to stay.

Objectives

Having said that aims are general targets then the specific outcomes are usually called 'objectives'. Using the analogy of the first-aid course, objectives could be:

By the end of the programme the participant will be able to:

- Administer artificial respiration
- Apply splints
- Control blood loss
- Clean and dress minor wounds

Note that we are stating exactly what the participants will be able to do at the end of the course and no more. This is extremely important in the design of training, as it is in many cases extremely important for a number of practical reasons that everyone knows exactly what training is supposed to be achieving. Often training goes wrong because objectives have not been stated or have been forgotten about in the design or delivery of training.

There are a number of technical and theroretical approaches to the design of objectives. Here I am looking at a simple and practical approach. Basically there are two types of objective:

1. Objectives which state what we have to do to show that we understand, are aware of, or know about (knowledge). These usually start with statements such as:

    By the end of the training programme the participant will:

    State the need for safety in...
    List the principles of...
    Describe how to...
    Explain how to carry out...

2. Objectives which state exactly what we will be able to do (skills). These normally start with statements such as:

    By the end of the training programme the participant will:
    Operate a turret lathe.

Analyse...
Be able to clean and dress minor wounds.

There is a clear distinction between these two types of objective. For instance we may know through training how a lathe works but this does not mean that we shall necessarily be able to operate one. If the objectives of the training say that we shall be able to operate a lathe then we should be able to do so.

Therefore when we are writing objectives we should be certain just exactly what the outcomes of a training course are expected to be. We must be certain that when we say that someone at the end of training will be able to do something, whether it be fly an aeroplane or write a business letter, that steps will be taken to ensure that these things can happen.

This usually means that when we are designing training in practical skills we should ensure every opportunity for participants to practise these skills. We also have to ensure that there are exercises and assessments of progress so that we can feed back to participants the progress they are making in acquiring the skills required.

By its very nature, an induction programme is an awareness-raising process. Therefore objectives will be of the first type. However, it is unlikely that we would actually test people on all these objectives and therefore the emphasis can be directed more towards what the trainer has to do.

I would suggest that objectives for an induction programme might look something like the following:

By the end of the induction programme the new entrant will have had explained:

1. The administration of salaries and pensions.
2. The company emergency procedures.
3. How the disciplinary and grievance procedures work.
4. The company organization.
5. How the training and development system works.
6. What steps the company is taking to ensure the satisfactory induction of each new entrant.

Although I have previously stated that the main objectives of an induction programme should be to commit and motivate by developing positive attitudes, you can hardly test these with new entrants. It is more important to write these for trainers as a form of 'hidden agenda'. For example:

7. Will be fully committed to remaining with the organization as long as mutually acceptable.
8. Will be committed to the culture within the organization and ready to work with colleagues as a member of a team.

Whether these last two objectives are explicitly stated or not, there should be no doubt in people's minds that induction is as much about committing and motivating as it is about informing. However, delivering information in an interesting way can be a vehicle for motivating new entrants.

Designing the Training

In Chapter 3 I looked at what can be included in the induction programme. One of the most important things is the *induction course*. The design of the training course can be crucial in establishing credibility for training and development and for committing the individual. Therefore a lot of thought should be given to designing a quality course which participants will enjoy and which will make them want to take part in further training.

One way to do this is to make the course both participative and *learner-centred*. This is simply jargon for basing the course on what the participants want and need to know rather than deluging them with everything and anything. It also means making sure that the content of the course is interesting and involves participants as much as possible.

But what kind of things make an induction programme or course interesting and stimulating? When I ask this on training-of-trainers or effective-presentation courses I invariably get the answer 'visual aids'. However, I have attended many presentations in which visual aids have been used but the presentations have still been dull and uninteresting.

Visual aids do not make for an interesting presentation. What makes a stimulating presentation is the wise use of a range of training media delivered in a participative manner. The training plan in Appendix 1 shows some examples of how audio-visual resources can be used in practice. The following is a range of resources which, when used at the right time and in the right way can add interest to the dullest subject. I shall be looking at training methods later on in this chapter.

Pre-recorded Audio-tapes

Some years ago I was given an audio tape by a training manager at Shetland Health Board. Shetland is twelve hours' sailing time from

Aberdeen and as near to Norway as it is to mainland Britain. When asked the location of their nearest main-line railway station when claiming expenses, Civil Servants in Shetland have been known to state 'Bergen'! It is indeed a very remote part of Great Britain and because of this there can be difficulties in recruiting particular skilled staff.

Shetland Health Board, at that time anyway, had difficulty in recruiting nurses. One solution was to produce a cassette tape. This was professionally done with one side being a musical and narrative introduction to Shetland. The second side is an introduction to nursing in Shetland and includes contributions from staff who have moved to Shetland to work. This tape was more of a method of recruitment by the Health Board but was also clearly a method of inducting potential employees to both working and living in Shetland.

Using this tape as a model, I have used tapes as a method of inducting participants on lengthy training courses to the course programme. It is a change from written material and is a more personal introduction if the person running the course actually produces the tape.

Slides and Photographs

When it is not possible for a participant to see every aspect of an organization during an induction course, or when there are aspects of an operation which take place at a different time of year, then one way of introducing participants to these aspects is through photographs, particularly slide photographs. I have experienced these being used effectively on a number of courses. However there are some guiding rules.

- Slide presentations should be based around the key points of a presentation; that is, choose the right slide to illustrate a point. Do not simply use any available slide because you have it.
- Slide presentations should be short and snappy. Long ones can bore an audience just as effectively as a long talk.
- Don't dwell unnecessarily long on each slide, but on the other hand, don't rush.
- Make sure slides are in order before showing.
- Rehearse!

Another effective way to make use of slides is to combine them with audio on a tape-slide production. I have seen this used to good purpose on a number of induction courses. Again the rules above apply. Obviously the extent to which this method can be used may be limited by resources available. However, it is amazing what can be done with just readily available domestic equipment.

Although it is not always possible, it can be more effective if employees or trainees are given a hand in producing the slide or tape-slide presentations. On one occasion I was responsible for organizing residential training courses for new, young recruits to a large organization. What I did was to get the young staff on these courses to learn the basics of photography and produce tape-slide programmes. These programmes worked well. Not only were they useful in developing new skills in staff, they were also successful in encouraging new staff to take up the residential places. This was mainly because they could learn at first hand about the course from some of their colleagues who had been on previous courses and who came along to the presentations to introduce to the new recruits the tape-slide programmes they had made.

Tape-slide programmes are particularly useful to cover such areas as personnel functions when different guest speakers may be delivering the presentation. If the programme is on tape-slide, the guest speaker can elaborate or simply respond to questions after the presentation.

Video Programmes

Although video is not always within the resources of some organizations, it is nevertheless a very useful method of presenting a wide range of information. I have also on one occasion seen a video of the chief executive of one national organization produced for use on courses throughout Great Britain. This had the effect of enabling the chief executive to greet new entrants and allowed the recruits to see and hear the chief executive.

Video has also been effectively used to induct staff into new developments in the organization. As above, video programmes can be more effective if they are produced by or involve staff within the organization. These should at the very least be consulted or used as advisers.

Due to the fact that induction is necessarily focused on specific organizations, it is well nigh impossible to come up with commercially produced videos which would be applicable. I have come across one which is an introduction to local authorities for young entrants, but this is about the only one. A reference is given at the end of the book.

Exhibitions and Displays

I remember, when visiting a regional Unemployment Benefit office, a display of artefacts relating to the history of the Department. When being given the responsibility for setting up an induction course in another region I used this idea and invited managers from throughout the region to search their storerooms and donate items we could use to set up a small museum. The result was totally unexpected because within a short period of time we had a small museum kitted out as an Unemployment Benefit office would have been in earlier years. During their induction training, all new entrants were able to see this exhibit. As part of the induction process was putting Unemployment Benefit into an historical and social context, this museum was invaluable in stimulating interest and helping entrants see the service as more than just a job, and as a social service. This philosophy is extremely important in such a government department.

Workbooks and Projects

A large national organization decided to offer a range of vocational qualifications to all of its several thousand workforce. As part of this process it decided to carry out induction briefings in the form of half-day seminars to introduce the awards. If the staff at these seminars decided to take up the qualifications they were issued with 'Induction Workbooks'.

These workbooks contained an open learning course in a loose-leaf form. The booklets introduced participants to the background to the awards and short exercises helped readers understand how the awards worked. Each workbook also included records of progress towards the achievement of the awards.

In a different industry, construction, I was involved in the design of what was called a 'work-based' project for young entrants to the industry. This project was used to help the entrants understand the safety and legal aspects of digging holes for municipal undertakings such as water, gas and electricity. The project was again an open learning one designed to help the trainees find out the answer to a range of questions by reading, asking questions, or having to carry out practical activities, sometimes under supervision. Here is an example of the kind of question that was asked:

> From whom would you seek permission to dig a hole in:
> a field?   a main road?
> a motorway?   a school playing field?

A major benefit of this project was that it introduced the entrants to the major aspects of health and safety in the environment in which they were working without their having to attend a training course. They were able to complete the project in their own time and at their own pace, and also wherever it was appropriate. It was specific to their occupation and completed the training gained on a general training course on health and safety in a construction environment. It also involved supervisors and colleagues, as the new entrant had to ask questions of them.

For the above reasons, workbooks and projects can be extremely effective in inducting new entrants to a range of subjects. However they should be used wisely along the following guidelines:

1. Workbooks should be well produced and readable.
2. They should be supported by supervisors, managers or appointed staff.
3. They should be properly introduced and explained.
4. They should be acceptable to the users and negotiated with them.

Of course we do not necessarily have to go to the lengths of producing detailed workbooks as above to make the induction enjoyable and participative. Simply by asking new entrants to find out things by themselves we can transfer the learning to them. For instance, there is a great difference between the following two examples:

1. The company nurse is situated on the second floor of block A next to the staff canteen.

And

2. Here is a blank map of the building. Find the company nurse and mark the location on the map. Put the name of the nurse in your induction checklist.

In the first instance we are giving information that may or not be retained. In the second, we are asking the entrants to find out for themselves. In this way the information is more likely to be retained. More than that, we are ensuring that the entrant meets the nurse. This transfer of the responsibility for learning to the learner can be used at any level and will be explored in more depth in the next chapter.

The Use of National Standards

In Chapter 9 I introduce the concept of 'national standards'. One of the main applications of national standards is in the design of training courses and programmes, using these standards to identify the key skills and knowledge inherent in a job or task. National standards are no less important to induction training, as they can be used as checklists to identify the 'must, should and could knows'.

There are national standards now covering most industries. The standards are in most cases specific to the industries and identify practical and technical skills and the knowledge and understanding required to practise those skills. They are of enormous benefit in the design of technical aspects of training.

National standards are described in terms of 'Units' and 'elements' of 'competence'. The simplest description of these are stand-alone 'chunks' of a job that describe the skills and knowledge required to carry out the job. 'Elements' are essential parts of the unit. 'Performance criteria' are statements of what the outcomes are when the unit has been performed competently. The 'range statement' explains the context in which the work is performed or the number of variables. For example, the range in the unit given below describes how 'respond to emergencies' covers fires, leakages and so on.

An example of a technical unit is given in Chapter 9. There are also more general standards that can be included on induction courses. For example, in the food and drink industry qualifications and in others, there are units covering such areas as the following:

- contribute to the health and safety of self and others
- maintain hygiene standards
- work with others.

If we look more closely at the requirements of one element of the health and safety unit we can see how training can be designed around the requirements of the element and how it can be made specific to the organization:

Unit Title – 1.1 Contribute to the health and safety of self and others
Element – 1.1.4 Respond to emergencies
Performance criteria

- Precautions are taken to protect self and others.
- Correct procedures are followed on discovering an emergency.
- Correct procedures are followed on being alerted to an emergency.
- Evacuation procedures are followed promptly.

Range statement

Emergencies to include fires, leakages, structural damage, major plant breakdown, injury to persons, power failure and bomb alert.

It can be seen how the above could be effectively used to design training courses that include simulations of incidents that may happen in the organization. The units can then be used as a checklist to ensure all aspects are covered. If used as the basis for qualifications, those staff being inducted and trained in health and safety issues would be assessed in the workplace and would have to demonstrate their ability, possibly through questioning and simulation, to respond to emergencies.

The potential for the use of national standards in training and development is enormous and I cannot do justice to it here. However, I have given references to appropriate texts. The essential point is that all those responsible for inducting new staff should familiarize themselves with the appropriate national standards both of a technical and a general nature so that induction and other training can be based on them.

EXAMPLE OF GOOD PRACTICE

One section of the food industry invested resources in researching the needs of staff and prepared a range of interesting and effective materials to introduce new qualifications to the complete workforce. This included leaflets to introduce the qualifications, customized workbooks and a tape-slide presentation tailored to various sectors of that industry. Presentation notes were also produced to assist presenters. In that sector, the take-up of the qualifications was high. This contrasted with other sectors where take-up was extremely low. In these sectors, no induction materials had been produced.

Designing to Standards

In Chapters 2 and 9 I have introduced the concept of national standards and Scottish and National Vocational Qualifications. Like other sectors, the training and development industry has its own lead body: the Training and Development Lead Body (TDLB). The TDLB has representatives from a wide range of training and development organizations and awarding bodies. The TDLB has produced a set of national standards from which are derived a range of qualifications for training and development specialists.

Like other standards, whether or not they are the basis for qualifications, they can also be used as the basis of the design of training courses and programmes. There are a number of units that may be applicable, but for the purposes of illustrating the principle I have selected one unit from the standards. It contains two elements and I have chosen the second to illustrate how the criteria can be used to measure whether a training session has been properly designed:

B22 Design training and development sessions

Element B221   Identify options for training and development sessions.

Element B222   Design training and development sessions for learners

Performance criteria
(a) Aims and objectives of the training and development are clearly specified.
(b) Opportunities for meeting learning needs are clearly specified.
(c) Methods of evaluating the effectiveness of the training and development sessions are clearly identified.
(d) Resources required to deliver the training and development session are clearly identified and secured.
(e) Training and development sessions effectively promote equality of opportunity.
(f) Training and development sessions utilize a range of techniques and activities.

It can be seen that the criteria above, which are statements of the outcomes when a task is completed competently, cover all the points that have been discussed in this and previous chapters. These criteria give a nationally accepted checklist for the designing of training and development courses and this naturally applies to induction courses. It is recommended that anyone with a remit to design induction training programmes should do so within the framework of the TDLB units and elements.

► **ACTIVITY**

Consider the work of your own department or section. If you could prioritize the must knows, should knows, and could knows, what would they be?

Part 2 DELIVERING INDUCTION TRAINING PROGRAMMES

5 Methods of Delivering Induction Training Programmes?

▷ **CHAPTER SUMMARY** ◁

- There are a number of methods of delivering induction programmes. These include:

Lectures	Simulation
Group discussion	Assignments and projects
Syndicate groups	Shadowing
Case studies	Literature, leaflets, handouts

- The most important thing with any of these methods is to make them participative and learner-centred. This motivates the learner and improves learning.

Learner-centred Methods

The training plan in Appendix 1 gives ideas on how to make the delivery of a training course participative and 'learner-centred'. By learner-centred we mean that we try to transfer the responsibility for learning from the teacher, trainer or presenter to the person who is being taught or trained. This is nothing new to many primary school teachers who have found that the best way to help children learn is to involve them in projects or other participative ways in lessons. Although rote learning of tables and alphabet still has its place, it has been shown that in such areas as history, geography and other practical subjects, involvement by the learner in the process speeds up learning.

As far as induction is concerned this does not necessarily mean that we involve participants in project work although it can be used where appropriate. In fact most methods of training and teaching can be learner-centred as long as we can accept the philosophy that the very best way to promote learning is to transfer the responsibility from the teacher to the learner. In effect the teacher or trainer becomes a 'facilitator', that is, someone who assists in the learning process but does not do it all.

The theory behind this is that if we give 'ownership' of the learning to the learner then he or she is more likely to retain the learning. For example if we are asked to carry out a piece of research and come up with something original, we are not likely to forget the details of what we have found. However, if we are told the same facts by someone else we are more likely to forget. But as far as induction is concerned, what does this mean in practice? It will be easier if we look at a range of training techniques and see how they can be made participative.

Lectures

If lectures or talks are considered as sermons, with one person talking to an audience, then this is hardly participative. If, however, we involve the audience, we can help them contribute to the learning process. This can be done by:

- Asking questions
- Inviting questions
- Putting forward hypothetical situations and asking participants how these can be tackled.

We should also be honest with ourselves in asking whether our presentations are boring. If we think they are, then we should take positive steps to make them interesting. This can be done in a number of ways, from attending training courses on effective presentation to examining every aspect of our presentations and asking in every case how we can transfer ownership of the learning to the learner. This can be very difficult for those who have been 'lecturing' for years but with practice it can be done. Appendix 1, A Sample Induction Training Course Programme, gives some examples.

Group Discussion

Group discussions are an effective way of involving participants if the discussion is managed effectively by a chairperson or group leader who can control the discussion and ensure that all those who want to can contribute. The leader can also ask direct questions. Discussion-leading is a skilled job, in that we are not simply talking about allowing an unstructured chat but managing a process in which each participant is allowed an equal contribution, and the leader is not necessarily putting a point of view but allowing other views to be fully discussed.

Syndicate Groups

Syndicate working is a way of putting the responsibility for solutions to problems in the hands of participants. It is even more effective if separate groups come up with different solutions and are allowed to debate them.

During an induction course for new Civil Servants, one of my tasks was to introduce these young entrants to the dreadfully dull details of how the Civil Service is funded and organized. What we did was to take all the key points (teaching points), and put them into illustrated folders. We then split the course participants into groups and asked each group to study the materials with a view to compiling 20 questions to be the basis of a quiz. The questions which one group came up with were asked of the other group and points were awarded.

This was an extremely effective method in a number of ways. First of all, the participants studied the materials seriously, being motivated by an interesting and participative outcome. During the quiz, the fact that the materials were discussed again meant that the learning was reinforced. There was therefore more chance that the learners would understand and appreciate the facts rather than listen to a boring talk and then immediately forget what had been said.

I have used group work of this nature with a range of participants on induction and on other courses. It needs close control and in some cases team-working of trainers to support the groups. It is, however, rewarding and productive.

Case Studies

Case studies are a good way of describing experiences and situations. They can be extremely participative if groups or individuals study the cases and are asked to come up with solutions to problems. On induction training you could possibly have an example of the lead-up to an accident at work. Participants could then be asked to say how it could have been avoided. By doing this they are storing the facts of the case in their memory. It is always more effective than simply hearing how an accident happened. Case studies could also be done on video or on tape-slide.

Assignments and Projects

This was also discussed in Chapter 4. It is a method which is particularly helpful with school-leavers and other young entrants in introducing them to new organizations. Assignments usually take the form of structured questions requiring them to find particular information relating to the organization or to their work. For instance, they may be required to find the location of the company nurse or first-aider. This is another way of giving the ownership of learning to the learner.

Simulation

In Chapter 4 I discussed the use of national standards in the design of training and I specifically mentioned how simulation could be used in the context of 'respond to emergencies'. Simulation is a form of training that can make a training course stimulating and enjoyable.

Simulation ranges from role-play situations on handling difficult customers to using highly sophisticated equipment such as flight and navigation simulators. The latter are used where the costs of the real thing are high or where the effects of any accidents would be dramatic. Simulation can also be used for events that are rare or unpredictable. They can be used effectively in induction training to train in such areas as health, safety and security or where other training is run in parallel, such as customer care. The techniques are probably best known through first-aid training.

A simulation can be used to train in emergency evacuation procedures when a fire alarm is set off and staff have to respond to it. At a higher level, more complicated simulation training is used for staff on oil drilling and production platforms where simulation also involves escape from a downed helicopter. In customer care it is used in exercises where staff are briefed to represent difficult customers who have to be dealt with effectively.

Simulations can range from the simple to the complex and in all cases it is necessary that training staff brief themselves and participants in what is expected of them, particularly if the simulation may have an impact on others such as in emergency procedures where other staff may have to evacuate.

> ### EXAMPLE OF GOOD PRACTICE
>
> One further education college has adopted the practice of inviting second-year students to induct first-year students. This involves assigning new students to a 'counsellor' who advises the student during the first two months. Second-year students also conduct visits round the college as well as presenting sessions on college rules and facilities. These presentations are assessed as part of the course work for the experienced students who are involved in media and communications skills training.

Delivering to Standards

In the previous chapter on design of programmes I introduced the TDLB standards and said how they could be applied to the design of courses, sessions and programmes. Not only do they apply to design but so too do they apply to delivery. A number of units are applicable and again I have chosen one unit and one element to illustrate.

C23   **Facilitate learning in groups through presentations and activities**

C231   **Give presentations to groups**

C232   Facilitate exercises and activities to promote learning in groups

Performance criteria

(a) The manner of presentation takes into account the size and composition of the group.

(b) Information is clear and accurate and presented in a tone, manner, pace and style appropriate to the needs and capabilities of the learners.

(c) Visual aids are legible, accurate and used in a manner which enhances the clarity of the information presented.

(d) Learners are encouraged to feel comfortable, to ask questions and make comments at appropriate stages in the presentation.

(e) Clear and accurate supplementary and summary information is provided on request and where appropriate to reinforce key learning points.

(f) Adjustments are made to the presentation in response to learners' needs.

(g) Distractions and interruptions are minimized wherever possible.

This is only a sample element and does not show the range of activities it would cover, neither does it show the evidence requirements if it were to be used within a qualification. It is given as an example to show that there are now specific and measurable standards against which anyone delivering an induction course or session can be assessed, whether or not that person is a training specialist, manager or occasional speaker.

Such standards are applicable to all other types of training and it is clear that if these standards are applied and evaluated then the overall quality of training courses is bound to rise. Again I would recommend that anyone involved in the design of induction training programmes should make reference to the appropriate TDLB standards.

Shadowing

Shadowing is popular in a number of organizations. This is a method whereby new entrants spend a certain amount of time with one or more members of staff finding out about the jobs they do. This gives new staff a feel for the organization and assists them in meeting a range of people. This has to be done cautiously as there is potential for new entrants to find themselves a bit spare if not given productive work.

Literature, Leaflets and Handouts

Having sat through induction sessions on things like pension schemes and superannuation, and then been given a leaflet on the same subject, I wondered what was the point, as the company should have realized that I could read. I don't suppose there is any harm in reinforcing the point but frankly, new entrants, especially young ones keen to join an organization, are not particularly riveted by talks from personnel officers on the superannuation scheme. Again it is a question of relevance and appropriateness. There are some subjects which are extremely difficult to make interesting on a course and which can be assigned to literature and leaflets so that new entrants can read them as required. On the other hand, there are trainers who can make any subject interesting in the way it is delivered. Therefore, if, when evaluating, we discover that trainees are not showing enough interest in one subject, then we should ask whether or not we could make it more interesting through the way in which it is delivered.

If we decide that it is more appropriate to put information in written form, either as the only way of communicating it or as a back-up, then it is important that the material is as professionally produced as possible. It might be less of an effort, but scrappy handouts copied from a copy tell a lot about the standards they can expect from the training centre.

▶ **ACTIVITY** ◀

If you give presentations or take part in training courses, consider the methods you use. Are there any ways in which you could transfer the responsibility for learning from you to the learner?

6 Skills, Knowledge and Attitudes for Delivering Induction Programmes

CHAPTER SUMMARY

- In order to deliver induction successfully, all staff who are involved should have the appropriate skills, knowledge and understanding.
- Priority skills are in the areas of communication, including presentation, listening, and questioning.
- Staff should also be able to design and deliver training effectively. This applies not only to those involved in courses and programmes but also to occasional speakers.

Skills, Knowledge and Attitudes Required

In Chapter 5 we discussed which people should be involved in the induction process. If these staff are to be involved then they should have particular skills to be able to carry out the induction properly and fully. They should certainly have a reasonable level of knowledge about induction processes and the organization. And they should have the right attitudes to want to carry that induction out professionally.

But what then are these skills, this knowledge and these attitudes? The list which appears below was compiled during a 'brainstorming' session at a seminar on designing induction. Obviously many of the aspects apply to more than just induction. I have chosen some of those I consider to be the most important in the delivery of the induction process. I discuss these in more detail after the lists.

SKILLS, KNOWLEDGE AND ATTITUDES
FOR DELIVERING INDUCTION TRAINING

SKILLS

listening
effective presentation
observation
questioning
oral skills
using audio-visual aids
problem-solving
writing skills
motivating

guidance and counselling
building confidence
selling skills
negotiating
managing groups
decision-making
organizing
assessing

KNOWLEDGE

structure of organization
  or programme
sources of referral and
  further information
resources for induction
self-knowledge
group dynamics
establishing training needs
knowledge of support systems
health and safety policy
equal opportunities policy
occupational knowledge
appropriate national standards

availability of courses
  and qualifications
welfare benefits
client group
life in general
appropriate legislation
special needs
effects of unemployment
people and behaviour
cultural and social
  relationships
effects of stress

ATTITUDES

polite
friendly
positive
helpful
non-judgemental
self-critical
committed
enthusiastic
approachable
encouraging
flexible/adaptable
honest

commitment to training
caring
respectful
confident
assertive
reliable
sense of humour
determination
objectivity
acceptable appearance
realistic

Key Skills for Delivering Induction

Communication Skills

Can we be sure that all personnel involved with new entrants have an adequate grasp of the ability to communicate clearly with others? In many cases supervisors have been appointed from the shop floor and may have been given little training in communicating with staff. Communication skills can include:

Listening	Observing
Speaking and presenting	Questioning
Guiding	

Listening Skills

We should always be aware of the barriers to good listening caused by:

Prejudice, eg colour, clothes, speech, accent.
Bias, eg through favouritism.
Interruptions, eg telephone, loud background noise.

At what level are we listening?

THE FOUR LEVELS OF LISTENING

1. At level one we are mechanically hearing.
2. At level two we are passively listening, that is, we are not showing that attention is being paid.
3. At level three we are actively listening and showing this by nodding our heads or making appropriate responses.
4. At level four we are hovering, that is we are pretending that we are an outside observer commenting on our own listening skills. Through this we can be objective about ourselves if we can honestly answer the following questions:
Is this person showing that he or she is listening?
Is this person prejudiced or biased?
Are there interruptions or is the interviewer being unnecessarily distracted?
I hear what is being said but is it what is being meant?
Is non-verbal behaviour being accurately interpreted?

Try this when you next have to talk to a colleague. If you can tell that you are not listening you can guarantee that your colleague can.

Speaking and Presenting Skills

When we are speaking to new entrants, whether on a one-to-one basis or to groups, is our language always:

clear
concise
uncluttered with jargon.

Are we speaking to inform rather than to impress? I have come upon trainers and managers who have been so full of their own importance that they have forgotten that the key to good speaking is to impress with the content rather than the speaker. However, delivery is important too. We can learn to make our speaking interesting by:

Not talking in a monotone
Varying our facial expressions
Illustrating
Putting in context
Using examples
Not boring with long talks.

One of the best ways to improve speaking ability is to both hear and see oneself on videotape. This is often an aspect of training courses on presentation skills or effective speaking.

Observing

In a sense this should possibly go along with listening skills because it is a form of listening, in that while interviewing or talking to new staff we should always be aware that facial expressions can give away a lot about what people are actually feeling. Being able to interpret those non-verbals accurately is a skill in itself.

Often the way we say things rather than what we say indicates how we feel, and we can in a sense easily expose ourselves to the skilled interviewer. This skill in observation is essential to guidance and it is one which can be acquired readily given one major condition: we have to be genuinely interested in the person we are talking to or counselling. To be able to observe properly we have to pay attention, and to do that we have to want to do so. So right away we have a difficulty, in that some staff may not particularly want to be involved with new recruits, and that would probably show in the way the recruits were dealt with. Therefore those people in the organization we choose to do the job must be the ones who want to do it.

Given that, we can then look at how we can best learn to observe. There have been a number of books written about interpreting non-verbal behaviour and these are possibly of some interest to the enthusiast. However, in my experience, by far the quickest way to learn how to interpret non-verbal behaviour, and especially facial expressions, is to pay attention and, in the same way as we hover when listening, to consider whether what is being said is in line with what we are observing. In that way, if we continue to make a practice of this we can automatically realize that what is being said is at odds with what is being meant.

In practical terms it can be used during induction or any other interviews with recruits to check that they are happy with what is happening to them. If we can identify problems through facial expressions then we can explore the problem further through questions. Which brings us to our next skill.

Questioning

The good interviewer needs not only to be able to listen properly both to what has been said and the way in which it is said. The interviewer also has to ask questions. These are most useful in that they provide the information we require. We can look at different questions:

The marathon question

The 'marathon' question is one which is favoured by some television presenters. This is a question which can either take the form of a statement or of a number of questions strung together, which leave the person being interviewed confused and wondering which question should be answered. The way to avoid this is to plan ahead exactly what you want to ask and stick to that question. If it works out that you have asked the wrong question, then follow up by asking the right question. Do not confuse the interviewee by changing horses in midstream.

The closed question

The 'closed' question is one which may receive only a 'yes' or 'no' answer. Although it is appropriate when you want a direct answer to a direct question it is not so useful when you are seeking information on which to base further questions. It is one to be avoided when you want full answers to a question.

The leading question

The 'leading' question is one which shows assumption and perhaps prejudice on the part of the person asking the question. For example: 'So you don't want to work any overtime?' is a question which smacks of assumption on the part of the person asking the question. It is generally asked when someone has already made up their mind what answer to expect. In this context we may want to ask a question which helps us explore why the person does not want to work overtime.

The open question

If we want to ask questions which allow us to examine responses in depth by listening and watching then we need to ask questions which give us information to expand on. These are called 'open questions'. For example: 'Why do you feel that you don't want to work overtime?' or 'Tell me what you have against overtime.' This last, although it takes the form of a statement is actually a question as it elicits information.

Open questions can take the form of a statement but more normally start with one of the following words:

What?	Why?
Where?	Who?
When?	How?

Along with the other skills mentioned above, questioning skills can be improved by attending training courses in interviewing skills which are generally available locally from training organizations.

These are only a sample from a long list of skills which anyone involved in induction might have. This book is not the place to look at each skill in depth. The intention is to show that certain skills, knowledge and attitudes are required, so that if they are missing then individuals can take steps to acquire them either through training, self-research, or simply examining their own attitudes and asking whether they are appropriate to dealing with new recruits.

EXAMPLE OF GOOD PRACTICE

One large engineering concern has taken induction so seriously that all training staff and managers who are involved in induction are required to attend a one-day workshop looking at the methods they should use to deliver it. If there are deficiencies in areas such as presentation or counselling skills, they are also encouraged to attend training in these areas.

Designing Training Courses

The design of induction training has already been covered in Chapter 4, and in Appendix 1 there is an example of a training programme for an induction course.

For those who have only an occasional part in speaking at induction courses then training in presentation skills or instructional techniques may be all that is required. Those training staff with a wider involvement in designing and delivering induction programmes should be well equipped with or working towards the widest range of the skills, knowledge and attitudes listed earlier in this chapter. They should also be fully conversant with the 'systematic approach to training' (sometimes called 'the training cycle') which is shown in its simple version in Figure 6.1.

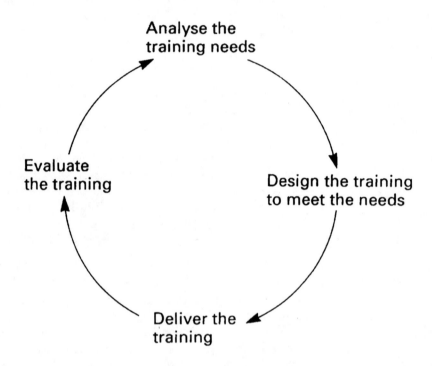

Figure 6.1 The training cycle

Most training-of-trainers courses are designed around the systematic approach to training and are geared to providing trainers with the skills to design and deliver training courses effectively. Such courses and qualifications are widely available throughout Great Britain from further education colleges and private providers. In Appendix 2 there is a checklist for those involved in organizing training courses.

ACTIVITY

Make a random selection of six each of the skills, knowledge and attitudes shown at the beginning of this chapter. To what extent do you effectively demonstrate these aspects? Is there scope for improvement? How can you take steps to improve these skills?

7 Roles in Induction – Who Carries it Out

▷   CHAPTER SUMMARY   ◁

The induction of new staff involves a number and variety of different people and departments in the organization. These include:

- The personnel department, which is responsible for induction through the recruitment process.
- Managers and supervisors who have the primary responsibility for training their own staff.
- Colleagues who can have officially delegated roles as mentors or unofficial roles through their positive attitudes to new staff.
- Staff representatives in representing new entrants and offering support.

Roles in Induction

This issue, more than any other, dictates the success or failure of an induction programme. In my experience, organizations, some of them fairly large, have concentrated their efforts at induction on the use of their training staff and in using central locations. Although training staff may be fairly experienced and knowledgeable, and training centres well equipped, the very existence of specific personnel responsible for induction can encourage those with the primary responsibility to duck out of it. In every case managers and supervisors have the primary responsibility for ensuring that training and development is carried out.

Nevertheless, the induction of new recruits is very often delegated to training staff, and these training staff very often assume that it is their primary responsibility. The point I want to make in this chapter is that induction of new recruits should be the responsibility of a number of people in any organization and not left solely to training staff.

The Personnel or Manpower Department

So where do we start? The first point of contact which a new member of staff has with any organization is with personnel sections and it is here that the first impressions are made. Therefore it is here that the first stages of induction should be carried out through informing and encouraging. As a central function, personnel or manpower departments, as they are sometimes called, are often detached from other departments and it is here that disenchantment can begin. Personnel is responsible for placing job advertisements and arranging interviews. These advertisements and interviews should properly reflect the job and all that is involved in it. Job descriptions have to be accurate and have been agreed by those in operating departments. It is most important that there should be a common understanding of new staff between those recruiting them and those managing them on a day-to-day basis. Later I shall be arguing that induction is part of an ongoing system, starting with the personnel function and ending with exit interviewing, probably carried out by the same department, in order to find out why personnel are leaving.

Managers and Supervisors

Managers and supervisors at every level have one of the most important roles in the induction of new staff. In many instances, managers and supervisors are neither briefed about new entrants nor are they trained in the processes of induction. Although these people can be encouraging about training and training staff they often look down on training as an unnecessary intrusion into the real work. Therefore it is essential that when we are developing managers and supervisors to encourage in them positive attitudes towards training in general and the training of new recruits in particular. We also have to give them information and training on how to go about the induction process and how to relate to others within the same process. This can be through induction checklists, review meetings, joint training courses or seminars. The main point is that managers and supervisors must be convinced of the need to carry out systematic and thorough induction programmes for their new staff and to encourage their other staff to be involved in the process.

Colleagues and Other Staff

While not wishing to protect new staff entirely from the influences of the more negative members of staff in your organization, the question is, if staff have negative attitudes towards the organization, should we know about these and take steps to do something about it? There is no point in covering up weaknesses and protecting new recruits from them. If we can use existing staff to identify weaknesses and protect new recruits from them this will in turn encourage new recruits to do the same. Therefore we can use the relationships between existing staff and new staff to a more positive end. Taking this a bit further, it is often a good idea to appoint selected positive individuals to be counsellors or mentors for new entrants until they find their feet. Clearly, the selection of such people is a delicate matter, as they themselves have to be convinced that it is a good idea. New entrants at every level need to be free to ask questions, question the organization and generally talk to somebody about what is going on. Having someone specific to do this helps to clear up a lot of initial reservations and worries new entrants have if they can be free to ask even the silliest question of someone they can trust. This concept of counselling or 'mentoring' has recently become more popular, particularly in relation to the concept of 'empowerment' and 'the learning organization'. I explore this in more detail in Chapter 9.

As induction should also give an overview of an organization, then staff in a wide variety of departments and functions may be called on to give presentations to new entrants on induction courses. Therefore these guest or occasional speakers should be prepared to contribute in an interesting way to such courses. If staff are asked to give such presentations then, if necessary, they should take steps to ensure they are able to do it competently, possibly by attending training courses on presentation skills. Training departments should also be prepared to offer such training either on a course programme or on demand. They can also suggest it to their guest presenters.

Staff representatives too should have a role in induction. If this is as guest speakers on induction courses they too should have access to training in presentation skills. Trade union representatives also have a role in supporting new entrants by introducing themselves and explaining how they can help and how they can be contacted whenever help is needed. Staff representatives should also be able to work along with personnel, training and departmental managers in reviewing turnover rates and improving induction programmes and courses.

The Training Staff

I have deliberately left the training staff to nearer the end of this list as I firmly believe that training staff must see themselves as fulfilling delegated roles in the induction process. Having said that, they do, however, have a major role in that process in facilitating the induction function and designing and delivering induction courses and programmes. So often in the past training staff have been isolated in training centres, carrying out short induction courses which very often are not particularly relevant to the organization and to the individual.

I have mentioned before having to put all new staff joining a Regional Council through a dreadful one-day course that included a slide show of living in the area. This was put on mainly for newcomers to the area, but those who had lived there all their lives were also expected to sit through it. Staff coming from different local authorities were also expected to sit through a session on how local authorities worked. No wonder it was questioned! This was a standard course that had been running for a number of years and had never been changed, basically because no one had asked participants what they had thought of it! Induction courses and programmes must be relevant to individuals joining organizations if they are not to feel like a number. If this has been happening in the past, training staff must ask themselves whether or not they should be more actively involved with personnel staff and managers to ensure that induction programmes are individualized and that courses are relevant.

Training staff are important to the induction function but it is of prime importance that they work alongside personnel, managers and supervisors to ensure that new entrants are going through individualized scheduled programmes at the most appropriate speed. In this chapter, I shall again be looking at this systematic approach to induction which involves staff in most departments of the organization.

Others

Induction is not a front-loaded procedure. It is not only appropriate when staff are brand new. It is the first point in a systematic integration of staff into the organization possibly lasting months or years. Since this is the case, then there must be a number of other staff involved in the process. Do all other employees, or customers for that matter, who have contact with new entrants know that this is a new person and therefore must be treated accordingly? It is a bit like treating a learner driver with a bit of consideration on the road. To take the analogy a stage further, isn't is a bit strange that learner drivers, after having passed their test, can go straight on to motorway driving and no one is required to give them more consideration than they do experienced drivers? On the other hand, I recently came across, in the Reo Stakis organization, new staff wearing badges saying 'Training to serve you'. It makes customers who notice the badges give a bit more consideration when being served by staff who are learning the ropes.

I am not suggesting for a moment that all new staff should wear badges to explain themselves. But it does point out that all new staff at the beginning of a new job or career may need support from all those with whom they are in contact at work. That may also mean informing customers and clients that staff are new to the job.

EXAMPLE OF GOOD PRACTICE

One company working in the food processing industry has taken the approach that all staff are involved in induction, and a session on this is contained in their customer care training. They see new staff as 'the internal customer'. The training involves approaches to introducing new staff and is based on the NVQ unit 'working with others', which is found in a number of qualifications.

▶ ACTIVITY ◀

Consider some of the new staff you or your department have recruited recently. Has it always been clear to customers and colleagues that these staff are new and are being inducted? Discuss with colleagues whether those with whom new staff are in contact need be informed about these recruits and if so how this is to be done.

If you are involved in education or in voluntary associations or clubs, discuss with associates whether new students or members are properly inducted and if not how it can be done. Discuss who would be involved in it.

8 Induction as Part of a Process

▷   CHAPTER SUMMARY   ◁

- Induction should not be seen to be in isolation, only acclimatizing the newcomer to the organization. Induction should be considered as part of an interlinked system starting with recruitment. This should be linked to induction and this in turn should be reviewed at staff appraisal. The system ends with exit guidance. Results from this should be fed back to find out whether we can more effectively influence staff to stay at an early stage. Staff involved in these processes should be trained in skills of interviewing, guidance and counselling.
- One way of integrating all aspects of induction is to consider new-entrant schemes that include policies on recruitment and induction.

The Employment Cycle

In previous chapters I said that induction should be part of a process. What I mean is that we should not look at induction in isolation, with little reference to what comes after it. We should look at induction as part of the 'employment cycle' which starts at recruitment and ends with exit interviewing as illustrated in Figure 8.1.

The employment cycle is closely related to the principals of Investors In People, which is explored in more detail in Chapter 9. Briefly, the Investors In People initiative recognizes organizations that commit themselves to the development of staff. This development is linked to business objectives and is evaluated on an ongoing basis. If it is recognized that development starts at recruitment then the process is, in the long term, easier to evaluate.

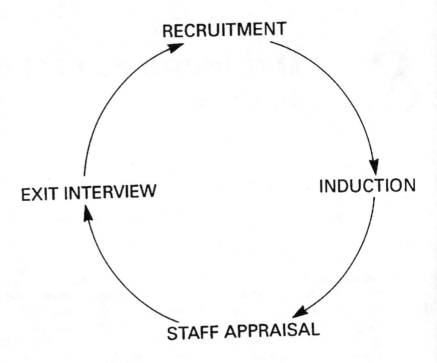

Figure 8.1 *The employment cycle*

Recruitment

If an organization is concerned to employ the best staff possible within its resources then it will naturally begin to sell the organization at the recruitment stage, starting most usually with the recruitment advertisement. A great deal of money can be spent on recruitment advertising and there is at least one national competition for the best recruitment advertisement.

A great deal is also spent on such recruitment methods as psychometric testing or straightforward interviewing and all its variations. And it is as this point, even before induction, that we begin to make the first impressions on the candidate we hope will be the new entrant. Not only do we expect the candidate to sell himself or herself to us, but we really are selling ourselves to the candidate.

It is strange that over the past two years I have heard of young people turning down jobs on the strength of the interviews they attended. This is because young people at school and on government training programmes are undergoing more and more training in attending interviews and preparing themselves for employment, and they know what to look for when attending interviews. They can tell what sort of employers it would be better not to have anything to do with. And it is these employers who do not know that it is they who are being interviewed.

So we have to decide that induction effectively starts at the recruitment stage and that we have to ensure that the way in which all prospective new entrants are treated at this stage is in line with our policy on induction. It would be particularly useful if those involved in the recruitment process also had some involvement in induction either as a guest speaker on induction courses or in later appraisal or review as discussed below.

Induction

As described in Chapter 3, induction is a process rather than a course. This being the case, how does induction relate to recruitment and to appraisal? First, it is important not to separate recruitment from the induction process. If we are able to build an integrated system, staff in personnel or manpower, who are responsible for terms and conditions and other things important to new entrants, will become familiar to them, so that they know whom to go to when there are problems.

This can be done by getting the appropriate personnel, for example, a welfare officer, to talk about the issues he or she can deal with. In this way the face is known and should then become more familiar. In many cases, induction courses are run by training staff who tell new recruits about terms and conditions. A better way is for the person responsible for the function to tell new staff about it. Unfortunately this has its hazards, if that member of personnel or other department is not a good trainer and cannot put over the message in an interesting way.

In one case I know of, guest speakers and other occasional speakers on central training courses were offered short courses on presentation skills because of the complaints about boredom from course participants. These short courses became very popular. As there are many staff who are called on to give presentations to many audiences but do not really know how to, it would be a good idea if such training were more widely available in organizations.

As previously stated, new entrants should be allowed to influence the organization. They will probably come with views of the organization from the outside and may be fresh and eager to get ahead. We have to respect this freshness and ask ourselves to what extent we should listen to newcomers and their ideas about our organizations. For instance, if I had been able to influence the second engineering company I worked for as described in Chapter 2, perhaps I would have stayed in that company longer. But it was clear to me, both from the general atmosphere and from listening to others, that the company was run by managers who were not interested in listening to staff but were content to follow their own road. It is interesting to note that that company, which for many years produced high quality optical and electronic equipment, had most of its products picked off one by one by imports and finally was taken over by a dynamic organization that overnight revolutionized management and staff relationships. I believe it is now a pleasant place to work. Although in this case it might have been only one of the reasons for the demise of this company I believe that the organization's inward-looking policy as illustrated by its treatment of staff, particularly in the first weeks of employment, had a lot to do with it. I usually find that companies with motivated and productive staff have systems of communication at all levels. This communication is best fostered right from the beginning, at induction.

Staff Appraisal and Review of Induction

If new staff start work on the basis of an individual induction programme which may last weeks or months, depending on the complexity of the job or organization, then it is only right that the individual objectives which have been laid out in the programme are reviewed at some stage to find out if they are being met. Therefore we have to build review into the process.

Although many organizations have staff appraisal systems very few have systems to review whether induction objectives have been met. It is my belief that over the first weeks or months of employment, staff appraisal should be centred around the difficulties staff have in acclimatizing to the organization. That means that appraisal forms should have a section that recognizes the need for the review of induction. This can be done by adding a section.

This should not be confused with a probationary report, which is generally concerned with work and conduct but no doubt could also include a section on how the entrant is acclimatizing to the organization. If the issues arising from a review of induction are dealt with at review then these, if not resolved, can easily be carried on to a regular staff appraisal system.

As discussed in Chapter 6, to carry out the induction process success-fully, including review, managers, supervisors and trainers should have the requisite skills. These skills can include counselling and interview-ing techniques which can readily be acquired on training courses.

If a staff appraisal system is not in place then it should possibly be considered, even for small organizations. Appraisal systems can be implemented, sometimes with the help of external consultants, and would normally involve fairly in-depth training and information sessions for all staff.

The Exit Interview

This is the final part of the employment cycle and to me it is an extremely important part. Having recently been asked to look at a proposed new-entrant scheme for a large organization, my first ques-tion was: 'Why do people leave?' This may seem to be starting at the wrong end. However, if you want to retain staff and commit individuals to the organization then you have to find out why they leave.

There are a number of reasons why people should leave any organi-zation and they are all legitimate: people moving house; moving area; moving with wife or husband; retiring, and so on. However, many people leave organizations for many reasons other than these. They leave because they are not satisfied with the organization. They may be depressed or stressed. Possibly they have not been getting on with certain individuals. Possibly their ideas are not being listened to. They may have domestic problems that they cannot cope with.

On the other hand, you hear supervisors or managers saying, 'You can't get people to stick to jobs these days,' or 'I'm glad to see the back of that one,' and 'He/she didn't last long'. It is a fact that many people leave employment very suddenly and often without explanation. In many cases the reasons given are sometimes not the real reasons. I have to admit that I have done the same myself as a younger person and felt guilty, ashamed and very low. With hindsight, few people could have blamed me, considering the treatment that I got from that particular company or from one particular individual.

Within the past few days I was talking to the manager of a large branch of a DIY chain who referred to the kind of staff he employed as 'dross'. In the same breath he complained about the turnover rate and how difficult it was to get these kind of people to deal effectively with customers. He also said that the company couldn't afford to train them. I would expect a high turnover rate in this organization. Not only because of the low wages but because of the lack of respect for the individual. I would also expect that many of these people would have little respect for management and would have few qualms in leaving without warning.

Had I been a director of that organization I would be concerned about the cost of recruitment, albeit low, given the fact that mainly unskilled staff were being recruited. It might indicate to me a low level of management skills. I would certainly want to monitor the turnover rate. In times of demographic change an organization like that will want to retain staff as much as it can. It should want to earn such a reputation as a good employer that staff will want to work there, rather than one that will always be considered a last resort.

Whether or not we are talking about high-volume turnover in semi- or unskilled work or an occasional departure in technical or professional occupations, we will want to know why people leave. Therefore there has to be a system to identify dissatisfaction at an early stage, and which can take steps to remedy this if necessary.

This dissatisfaction can be picked up during review of induction or at staff appraisal. Failing this it can be picked up if there is an opportunity to interview staff when they have decided to leave. This means that there have to be, first of all, administrative systems that identify leavers at, say, local offices or depots and feed back the information to the personnel section.

There also have to be the right people to carry out exit interviews. As many people leave because of relationships with immediate supervisors or managers, there should be a facility for an independent person to carry out the interview.

The interviewer should be skilled enough to carry out an in-depth probing interview to determine whether the reasons given for leaving are actually the right reasons. The reasons can then be recorded and categorized under the headings shown in Table 8.1.

To be effective, any results of such an exit interview should be fed back to those most able to make use of them. If the results over a period of time show that turnover is to do with manager-staff relationships then this can possibly be resolved through team-building or other routes to management development. It may call for a complete review of the way managers handle staff.

If the results show that a disproportionate amount of staff are leaving because of the salary or other conditions then it may be time for a salary review.

If staff are leaving because of poor promotion or lack of development or for any other reason we should be asking why these things

Table 8.1 *Exit interview – aide-mémoire*

Relationships	Did the interview indicate that there was a poor relationship between leaver and superior? Was there an indication that the leaver did not get on with colleagues? Why?
Finance	Is the leaver concerned about: – Salary or wages? – Expenses? – Pension?
Conditions	Is the leaver concerned about working conditions? Which?
Personal	Are there domestic or personal reasons for leaving? What are they?
Promotion	Is there any indication that promotion or career development prospects have not been realized?
Training	Is there an indication that the leaver has not received appropriate training?
Other	Are there other reasons why this person is leaving?

have not been picked up during staff appraisal and fed back to the appropriate managers or departments. One way to do this, depending on the size of the organization, is to have a committee or group which analyses the results of such exit interviews and makes recommendations on how the organization can encourage staff to stay. This committee could also analyse the results of such exit interviews and may involve:

- Director or senior staff who would chair and ask searching questions.
- Training staff who can comment on lack of training or development and who would feed back information to staff involved in induction training.
- Personnel staff who can comment on terms and conditions.
- Staff representatives to comment on staff concerns.

Clearly, one would not expect such meetings to be particularly regular unless the organization was big and turnover was excessive. If regular meetings are not necessary then there should at least be a member of staff responsible for monitoring turnover and reporting when it reaches a level for concern.

It would be ideal if one person had complete control of liaison between those responsible for induction, staff appraisal, and exit interviewing. This would ensure a consistency of approach and make sure that all involved were aware of all of the issues and concerns and were in a position to take action on them.

A New-entrant Scheme

One way to look at the recruitment of new entrants to an organization is through a new-entrant scheme. This would integrate all aspects of the employment cycle by committing the organization to a policy for all new entrants. This would possibly include:

A Policy for Recruitment

This would state which kind of staff are to be recruited. A decision might be made to concentrate on women returners or more mature workers. It might result in consideration of the need to recruit abroad in the light of greater European integration and the need to have those with language skills to deal with customers or contacts in other countries.

We can only target the right categories of employee if we monitor the outside environment and debate the issues involved. This can be done if we implement a recruitment policy and set up a team to monitor it.

A Policy for Induction

Based on the guidelines in this book, this would state:

1. That the organization is committed to full induction for all new entrants.
2. That every new member of the organization would have an individual induction programme drawn up.
3. That every new member of staff would have access to comprehensive and appropriate induction.
4. That as part of the induction process, each new member of staff would have the opportunity to discuss a training plan to meet agreed needs.
5. That every entrant would be given an opportunity to discuss aspects of induction at staff appraisal and exit interviewing.
6. That all those involved in induction will receive appropriate training to carry out induction.

7. That a review team would be set up to monitor all aspects of the induction policy.

A coordinating and review body would have a remit to implement a new-entrant policy and review every part of it. It would be involved in reviewing aspects of staff appraisal relating to induction and also the results of exit interviews.

EXAMPLE OF GOOD PRACTICE

One large Irish company has a 'Charter for Training', which includes a statement on the depth of induction each grade of new recruit will receive. This includes:

◇ a statement on induction course content
◇ a statement on responsibilities for induction
◇ timescales for review
◇ a policy on determining individual training needs.

► **ACTIVITY** ◄

Consider some of the staff who have left your organization over the past few months. Using the *aide-mémoire* in this chapter as a guide, do you think there were problems that, if you had known about them at the time, you could have taken action on which could have resulted in those staff being retained?

9 New Issues in Induction?

> ◁ CHAPTER SUMMARY ▷

- There have been a number of new issues arising that will have an effect on the content of induction training programmes. The Investors In People award requires that organizations carry out systematic induction, while the new National and Scottish Vocational Qualifications require proper introduction for candidates, whether or not they are new to the organization.
- The concepts of empowerment and the learning company have implications for the content of induction programmes in that they can be a very new concept and may need sensitive but planned implementation.
- Quality management is also becoming more important and it is essential that new staff understand the requirements of the adopted quality management system.

New Approaches in Training and Development

Since this book was first published in 1991, a number of new initiatives and approaches to training and developing staff have emerged or, having been developed, are now being more widely recognized as having practical importance. Two of these initiatives, Investors In People and National and Scottish Vocational Qualifications are based on specific structured standards while the other two discussed, mentoring and empowerment, have grown out of a developing school of thought that recognizes the importance of personal growth and the contribution it can make to team and personal development. These initiatives are summarized here with further references given in the Bibliography.

Additionally, the quality movement is growing, with more organizations implementing quality management systems such as Total Quality Management (TQM) or BS5750/ISO9000. It is vital that the new recruit is aware of these initiatives and how they may affect the way in which they work.

Investors In People

This is a government initiative designed to recognize those organizations committed to business success through staff development. It starts with the identification of long-term business goals and then asks for a commitment to the long-term management, training and development which will meet these goals.

Investors In People (or IIP) is based on a national standard comprising four principles:

Commitment. An Investor In People makes a public commitment from the top to develop all employees to achieve its business objectives.

Review. An Investor In People regularly reviews the training and development needs of all employees to achieve its business objectives.

Action. An Investor In People takes action to train and develop individuals on recruitment and throughout their employment.

Evaluation. An Investor In People evaluates the investment in training and development to assess achievement and improve future effectiveness.

Each of these principles has a number of indicators against which an organization is independently assessed to determine whether that organization is an Investor In People. Having achieved the award, organizations are then free to use the logo on their letterheads or recruitment advertising to show potential recruits that they are committed to staff development.

The principles referred to are not new, being based on the training cycle discussed in Chapter 6. What is new is that it is a national award recognizing those organizations who are using the best and most cost-effective means of training and development. It encourages organizations to look at whether the training and development provided is truly linked to business objectives and is therefore contributing to business success.

In terms of induction training, Investors In People is extremely important. Within the third principle, the following indicators appear:

3.1. All new employees are introduced effectively to the organization and are given the training and development they need to do their jobs.

3.3. All employees are made aware of the development opportunities open to them.

3.4. All employees are encouraged to help identify and meet their job-related development needs.

So for the first time there is a process to measure whether effective induction is taking place. These indicators along with others will be examined to determine whether the organization is meeting the standard through systematic induction which includes introductions to the organization and the identification of training and development needs linked to the business plan.

The Investors In People initiative is managed at a local level by Training and Enterprise Councils (TECs) in England and Wales and by Local Enterprise Companies (LECs) in Scotland. Details of these are in local telephone directories; information is also available from: The Employment Department, Moorfoot, Sheffield, S1 4PQ.

National and Scottish Vocational Qualifications

In the history of training and development, National and Scottish Vocational Qualification (N/SVQs) are probably having as big an impact as any previous initiative. They are revolutionizing training and development design.

The new qualifications are based on national standards. These standards have been developed by virtually every sector of industry and are laid out in a common format described in 'units' and 'elements of competence' along with their associated performance criteria. Here is an example of one unit from the N/SVQ in Administration that is common to most industries. This example gives only one selected element:

Unit 7   Prepare documents
Element 7.1   Respond to correspondence
Performance criteria
(a) Correspondence received for own reply is correctly identified.
(b) Correspondence received outside own responsibility is routed promptly to correct person.

(c) The speed, mode and cost of the reply reflect its urgency and importance.

(d) The correct meaning and tone of the response are accurately conveyed by the language and grammar used.

(e) Response is accurate, clear and in the style of the organization.

(f) Copies of correspondence and replies are stored in accordance with organizational procedures.

(g) Procedures for the security and confidentiality of data are in accordance with organizational requirements.

These national standards have wide application not only in the design of training and development programmes and vocational qualifications; they can also be used in the design of job descriptions and employee specifications as well as other personnel applications.

The new qualifications based on the standards depend on the assessment of competence demonstrated in the workplace. This competence is assessed by trained and qualified assessors.

Some organizations are making these qualifications available to all staff and are introducing them at the induction stage. If the qualifications are being promoted then it is necessary that they be properly introduced to staff. They should then be built into individual development plans as part of the induction process. Any introduction would include:

- A background to N/SVQs and national standards
- The N/SVQs appropriate to the industry/job
- How assessment will be carried out
- Who will assess.

In the Administration qualifications is the unit 'Develop self to improve performance'. This unit appears in other qualifications but is an ideal one for the purposes of induction as it encompasses the identification of training needs and agreeing a plan to ensure that these needs are met. It is a formal way of ensuring that induction is being carried out and that it is based on training needs, including the need to be properly introduced to the organization and to the new qualifications.

Mentoring

Mentoring has in recent years been seen as a powerful tool in staff development, particularly when linked to the concepts of empowerment discussed below. Mentoring is a support system wherein staff new to the organization, new to a department, new to the job or involved in radical change are assisted in coping with the changes through the support of objective and independent third parties.

For instance, one major organization in Scotland whose managers were involved in a management development programme as well as phased restructuring over a period of years, was helped through this by independent consultants appointed to support these managers. This mainly involved listening to the managers and helping them see how the new management skills being learned could be applied in the organization and how they could deal with specific staff and organizational problems caused by the restructuring.

One organization uses the concept of mentoring to assist graduates new to the organization who are also pursuing MBA programmes. The organization recognizes the pressures which these new staff are under and that they need specific senior staff whom they can approach with a whole range of problems including those related to their course work and in-house projects.

Other functions of a mentor might be:

Counselling	Offering career advice
Coaching	Listening
Setting an example	Advising on professional development
Encouraging	Sharing expert knowledge.

The principles of mentoring are relatively simple: staff undergoing change are under pressure, but they can be assisted through these changes by independent persons who understand the pressures and can therefore provide support.

With the introduction of competence-based programmes, as discussed above in N/SVQ development, the need for in-house support is increasingly being recognized. In many instances, line managers do not have the time or the support skills to help their staff through the new qualifications. This can be an instance when a mentor is useful.

But mentoring is not a haphazard allocation of a new member of staff to a more senior person. Although mentoring can range from a very informal to a structured formal approach, it is necessary to consider carefully the implications of using mentors and whether it is necessary to implement a recognized programme including identification and training of mentors.

Mentors and those being mentored should be well matched. One mentoring consultancy allows those being supported to choose a consultant after an introductory workshop. Mentors should be volunteers and should be properly trained, with appropriate interpersonal skills such as listening.

The mentoring programme should be seen to have the support of senior management. Issues raised as a product of mentoring should be seen to be acted upon, if not confidential. The limits of confidentiality should be established, as should be the role and remit of mentors.

There are a number of other issues to be considered before implementation and I have given references in the Bibliography to specific guidance on the subject.

In terms of induction, mentoring is probably one of the quickest ways to help new staff at any level adjust to their new organization or circumstances, with the mentor taking less of a role as the new recruit settles in.

Empowerment and 'the learning organization'

The concept of empowerment, although not new to some enlightened organizations, has become increasingly important over the past few years, particularly in relation to National and Scottish Vocational Qualifications and Investors In People.

Empowerment is simple and straightforward in its intention, although possibly not so in its implementation, as it means the shifting of power from traditional managers to teams and individuals. It means that staff are encouraged to take initiative, problem solve and think for themselves.

In order to encourage empowerment, managers have to give up power and control over their staff. If properly conducted, this should then lead to increased motivation and effectiveness. It encourages team development and consultation. There are two main principles:

- Managers should be prepared to allow staff the freedom to take decisions appropriate to their level of competence, knowledge and authority.
- Staff should be prepared to accept this responsibility and be accountable.

In the development of an empowered organization, teamworking becomes important. If individuals are to take on responsibility then they need to discuss issues with their peers in order to make informed decisions.

The organization may have to prepare itself for what can be a fundamental shift in its cultural attitude. It is also clear from experience that not all managers may enjoy what might be seen as a stripping of their power. For this reason, any move towards empowerment should be prepared for and should start with agreement from those being empowered and then move on to development programmes which help staff through the transition.

In terms of induction, it is clearly necessary to assist new staff come to terms with what may be a dramatic cultural shift to them if they have been working in a traditional organization where power and control has not been delegated. This briefing may also need to include introductions to the team and to teamworking if such is the culture.

Related to empowerment is the concept of the 'learning organization'. A learning organization is one in which all aspects of learning are encouraged at all levels. The personal growth referred to previously is further developed in that staff are encouraged to take responsibility for their own development and resources are made available for this. One organization has taken the first steps in this by briefing all staff on the wide range of opportunities available to them and then making managers responsible for training budgets, so moving responsibility from the training department to individuals and teams where the organization believes it belongs.

The learning organization is characterized by staff who, at all levels, have the opportunity to get involved in policy formulation and strategy, whose views are taken into account, who interact with suppliers and customers and who see themselves as part of the whole rather than as a member of a specific department.

In common with other initiatives, we cannot assume that all recruits will want to share the implied values, let alone understand them. The recruitment process should address the former in the sense that those being recruited should be aware of the values and culture within the organization. If they make the choice to join, they should then be properly inducted into the ways they can be helped develop and how they can contribute to the learning of others and of the organization.

Quality Initiatives

More and more, local and national press reports and advertisements feature organizations that have achieved accreditation under the British Standards Institution quality accreditation, BS5750 or its International equivalent, ISO9000. These quality awards are based on criteria laid down by the British Standards Institution and are assessed by accredited assessors.

Other organizations are approaching quality control through their own in-company schemes, which may or not incorporate BS5750/ISO9000. Total Quality Management (TQM) is an approach that encompasses every aspect of quality improvement within an organization. Such TQM schemes are often customized and given names specific to the organization.

'Benchmarking' is a quality system that identifies practices, services and processes in the best organizations and strives to emulate these. This movement is gaining ground and articles on its implementation are increasingly being seen in management and training journals.

'Chartermark' is a quality system specific to government and public bodies such as utility companies. Chartermark is primarily based on customer service standards. One development agency has benchmarked the best customer service standards and is using these to produce statements of the quality which it will apply to its customer care.

Whether quality is managed through BS5750/ISO9000, TQM, benchmarking or Chartermark, there is a requirement to ensure that staff are fully introduced to the adopted approach and are trained in the use of the quality systems as well as the necessary paperwork. For existing employees this would be through a specific training programme, while for new employees it would be necessary to incorporate elements of the training within the induction programme. Such issues to be addressed might be:

- The need for quality management
- What is ISO9000/BS5750/TQM/benchmarking/Chartermark?
- The use of the quality manual
- Documents and procedures
- Conformance and non-conformance.

Conclusion

It has often been said that there is really nothing new in training and development in that what seem to be new approaches have been around for some time in different guises, or used by a small number of people, or simply given a new name. This may or not be true, but what is true is that, for the first time, through the initiatives above, there are specific standards against which these training and development programmes can be measured. It is in this light that induction has become more and more necessary, not only for the training professional, but for managers and supervisors, for the personnel department and for the quality manager. Induction is taking on an importance that it has not had before and it is therefore vital that it is treated as critical and designed and delivered to the highest professional standards.

EXAMPLE OF GOOD PRACTICE

One organization has fully embraced the concept of mentoring by asking some of its newly retired staff to return occasionally or to be on call to help new members of staff acclimatize. There is a retired staff association and they are now running courses to help these retired staff members carry out effective mentoring and induction. This has a motivating effect on all staff, not least the new recruits and those who are retired.

► **ACTIVITY** ◄

Consider the culture in your organization. Is there scope for looking at any or all of these new initiatives? If you already have, are these reflected in the content of the induction programme? An induction programme must change with the culture and recognize new developments.

Have you considered implementing a system of quality management, and is this addressed in your induction programme?

Appendix 1:
A Sample Induction Training Course Programme

AIMS: This training course is designed to introduce new entrants to the company and to ensure a full integration through introducing them to the more important company policies and practices.

OBJECTIVES: By the end of the course the participants will have had explained to them:

1. The background, structure and future developments of the company.
2. The company health and safety policy and be committed both to working in and maintaining a safe and healthy working environment.
3. The company security system and their personal roles in maintaining security.
4. Qualifications and the opportunities to achieve these.
5. All relevant personnel and administrative matters.
6. The staff associations and clubs.

DESIGNED FOR: All junior entrants to the head office and branches of the .... Company.

LENGTH OF COURSE: Two days.

DATES: 5 and 6 Oct. 19–

INDUCTION TRAINING COURSE
COURSE PROGRAMME

DAY 1
09.00   WELCOME AND INTRODUCTIONS
This should be an ice-breaking exercise designed to encourage participants to get to know one another. Ask each person to interview the person next to them. They should be briefed to ask:

> Names
> Where they come from
> Which office they work in
> What their duties are
> Hobbies, sports, interests.

Give 15 minutes for this. While this is going on, issue name badges and ask them to put their names on. At the end of this time ask them to introduce one another on the basis of the information they have gathered.

This should be informal and light-hearted, as it should set the tone for the rest of the course.

Alternative: Put participants into small groups to introduce themselves and have one person representing each group feed back details in plenary (large group).

10.00   WELCOME
This is a formal welcome to the company by the head of personnel and training, Jean Dickinson. It will be followed by a tea-break during which Jean will chat to the new entrants.

11.00   THE ... COMPANY
This is an introduction to the company covering history, geography and future developments.

This is a tape-slide programme especially produced for this course. It features a number of local offices and their staff whom entrants will probably recognize.

When the programme is over take participants to the small display featuring 'Life in the Company through the years'. Discuss the changes:

> Working conditions
> Communications

Staffing – more women
Information technology.

This session is intended to show that while the company is keeping up with the times it is also ensuring that staff conditions are keeping up-to-date.

12.00   CONDITIONS OF EMPLOYMENT

The above should lead neatly into this session which is a presentation by the personnel section on the main issues to do with terms and conditions of employment:

1. Introduction by tutor to personnel representative.
2. Welfare – a handout of three case studies of how individuals have needed help and got it.
3. Pension – a short talk only, unless there are questions. Issue information booklet.
4. Discipline – a presentation based on the need for standards, especially when dealing with the public. Ask entrants what standards of discipline they think should be applied. Give copies of procedures.
5. Grievances – as above.
6. General discussion. Ask if there are other issues. Stress that there will be time during individual interviews to talk over any worries or concerns.

13.00   LUNCH with training staff in staff canteen.

14.00   HEALTH AND SAFETY

On return from lunch, put all into small groups. Explain that they will now be shown a film of a company office during a normal working day. Tell them that after seeing the film they will, in groups, be asked to identify the things in the film which they consider to be unsafe or dangerous.

In plenary, ask groups to report back. Put lists on a flipchart and discuss.

On overhead projector (OHP) show the main points of the Health and Safety Act and discuss. Give out Health and Safety Act leaflet and discuss. Give out copies of the company Health and Safety Workbook. Explain that these should be completed and discussed with supervisors who will also be going over the induction checklists when entrants return to their departments or offices.

16.00   OPEN DISCUSSION AND REVIEW

This session should review the work done during the

day. Discussion should centre on any worries and concerns the entrants have.

16.45   CLOSE

DAY 2

09.00   WELCOME BACK

Ask if there are any issues arising from yesterday and discuss.

09.30   DEALING WITH THE PUBLIC

Although there will be a forthcoming 'Dealing with the Public' course, this session is used to introduce the major points. Put into syndicate groups and ask them to answer the question:

> 'What standards of behaviour, dress and appearance do you think the public expects of staff in this company?

Give 40 minutes in groups. Ensure groups are monitored to make sure they are addressing the issues. On return ask for feedback. Put on flipchart major points to be covered:

Dress	smart (shirt and tie for men) up-to-date but not outrageous clean.
Appearance	clean hair fingernails clean.
Conduct	timekeeping attitudes to public getting on with others.

10.30   STANDARDS AND QUALIFICATIONS

This session is designed to introduce new entrants to the company's newly established standards and the company-sponsored qualifications it may be useful to acquire. Show the Training Agency Video: Standards for Success.
Give out copies of the standards. Ask them to find examples applicable to their work. Explain that qualifications will be assessed in the workplace and supervisors will receive training to do this.

11.30   TRAINING AND DEVELOPMENT

Explain that besides making the new qualifications available, the company wants to invest in staff development.

This can take the form of training courses run in-house or longer courses at colleges of further education or polytechnics. Each new entrant will be offered training that will be agreed at a meeting with the training section within the first three months. In the meantime ask participants to begin to consider what training might be applicable.

Show the short video case studies of staff who have taken up training and development opportunities. Discuss.

On the way to lunch show participants the reference library which they can have access to at any time for study and research.

12.30	LUNCH in staff canteen.
13.30	TOUR OF HEAD OFFICE

On return from lunch brief entrants that they are about to go on a tour of head office. Each section head has been briefed to give a short display or presentation about the work of the section. These will be in a number of formats:

Talk
Exhibition
Tape-slide

The tour will include a visit to security where they will see a short video on personal security.

We shall go round in groups and each group will be led by a head office staff member. To make it more interesting, on return, each group will be asked the same 20 questions based on the tour. So everyone had better listen hard!

On return ask the groups the questions in plenary, and score. Put questions and answers on flipchart and make sure any wrong answers are corrected.

Give out:

Company directories
Map of local offices
Organizational charts

15.30   STAFF ASSOCIATION AND CLUB

This is a discussion and presentation by a staff association representative. The discussion should be based on what participants would look for from an association that is supposed to represent them. Discuss benefits of belonging to the association. Give out application forms.

Discuss staff club, and facilities and activities available. Give handout.

16.15   REVIEW AND CLOSE

This session should review the work of the two days. Discuss and give out evaluation sheets, which should be returned through section heads.

The course will be closed by the head of personnel and training, Jean Dickinson.

Appendix 2: Checklist for Planning a Training Course

MARKETING
- Does the course have to be advertised?
- Has it been advertised well enough in advance?
- Are the advertisements of the right size and in the most relevant publications?
- Do information sheets or brochures need to be produced?
- Has a mailshot been considered and implemented?
- Have interested parties been targeted and approached?
- Does the course appear on a programme or newsletter and has it been distributed as appropriate?

ACCOMMODATION
- Have appropriate rooms been booked?
- Are the rooms big enough for all course activities?
- Is the level of heating appropriate throughout the venue?
- Is the light right for slides, overhead projector?
- Is blackout material available if required?
- Is the sound right?
- Do you need amplification?
- Are there enough seats?
- Are the seats comfortable enough for the whole period of the course?
- Are tables available?
- Are there facilities for group work?

- Are adequate power points available?
- Do you know the domestic arrangements?:
  Coffee/tea/etc
  Lunch
  Overnight arrangements if residential
  Toilets and rest rooms
  Fire escapes
  Emergency drills.

- Have you considered possible interruption and guarded against it:
  Telephones in training room
  Noise from adjoining rooms
  Noise from outside
  Unrestricted entry?

JOINING

- Do you need a pre-course questionnaire?
- Do participants need to bring anything?
- Do they need to do any pre-course work?
- Have you sent joining instructions:
  A map
  Details of how to get to venue
  Details of start/finish times
  Train/plane times
  Dietary requirements
  Names of course leaders
  Contact address and telephone numbers
  Has attendance been confirmed?

RESOURCING

- Do you have:
  A course training plan
  A course folder including register of participants
  Handouts as appropriate?
- Hardware:
  Overhead projectors
  Slide projectors
  Projector stands
  Spare bulbs
  Screen of appropriate size
  Video recorders
  Monitors

Flipchart stands
Whiteboard
Video cameras
Microphones
Microphone clips or stands
Earphones
Appropriate leads
Extension leads/adaptors
Photocopier if required.

- Consumables:
Video tapes
Audio tapes
OHP acetates
OHP pens
Whiteboard pens
Board cleaner
Flipchart paper
Flipchart pens
Pens/pencils
Paper
Folders
Name cards or badges
Blutak

FINANCIAL

- How are the training facilities to be paid for?
- Has VAT been taken into account?
- How are participants to pay:
Cash
Cheque
Invoice?

OTHER

- Are you aware of participants with special needs and have you prepared for them?
- Are the training rooms prepared:
Seating
Audio-visuals
Handouts?
- Are the rooms neat and tidy?
- Is the preparation completely professional?

Select Bibliography

(Place of publication London unless otherwise stated.)

ACAS (1985) *Induction of New Employees* – Advisory Booklet No. 7.

ACAS (1988) *Labour Turnover* – Advisory Booklet No. 4.

ARMSTRONG, M (1993) *A Handbook of Personnel Management Practice*, Kogan Page.

ARNOLD, J (1986) 'Getting Started – How Graduates adjust to Employment', *Personnel Review*, 15(1).

BOURNER, T & BARLOW, J (1993) *The Student Induction Handbook*, Kogan Page.

BROWN, R & BROWN, M (1994) *Empowered*, Nicholas Brealey.

BUCKLEY, R & CAPLE, J (1989) *The Theory and Practice of Training*, Kogan Page.

CITB (1981) *Induction Training*, Training Information Guide XA610, Bircham Newton.

EMPLOYMENT SERVICE (1988) *Code of Practice on the Employment of Disabled People*, Sheffield.

EQUAL OPPORTUNITIES COMMISSION (1985) *Code of Practice for the Elimination of Discrimination on the Grounds of Sex or Marriage and the promotion of equality of opportunity in employment*, HMSO.

EQUAL OPPORTUNITIES COMMISSION (1987) *Signposts: A Guide for Women Returning to Work or Learning*.

FLETCHER, SHIRLEY (1994) *NVQs Standards and Competence*, Kogan Page.

FOWLER, A (1983) *Getting Off to a Good Start: Successful Employee Induction*, Institute of Personnel Management.

GAPPER, JOHN (1990) *Fifty Plus: The Importance of Mature Workers in the 1990s*, Reed Employment.

HOPSON, B & SCALLY, M (1976) *Lifeskills Teaching*, Maidenhead, McGraw-Hill.

INDUSTRIAL SOCIETY (1984) *Notes for Managers – Induction.*

JACKSON, P & ASHTON, D (1993) *Implementing quality through BS5750/ISO9000*, Kogan Page.

JONES, D F (1984) 'Developing a new Employee Orientation Programme', *Personnel Journal*, March.

JONES, R A (1982) 'Setting Standards for New Employees', *Supervisory Management*, June.

KAKABADSE, A, *et al* (1988) *Working In Organizations*, Penguin Business Books.

LEECH, T (1985) *How to Prepare, Stage and Deliver Winning Presentations*, Amacom.

LLOYD, C & COOK, AMANDA (1993) *Implementing Standards of Competence*, Kogan Page.

MACKAY, I (1980) *A Guide to Asking Questions*, BACIE.

MACKAY, I (1984) *A Guide to Listening*, BACIE.

MADDUN, R B (1988) *Effective Performance Appraisals*, Kogan Page.

PARSLOE, E (1995) *Coaching, Mentoring and Assessing*, Kogan Page.

PEDLER, M, *et al.* (1991) *The Learning Company*, McGraw-Hill.

PORTER, I W, *et al* (1987) *Behaviour in Organizations*, Singapore, McGraw-Hill.

ROTHERY, B (1993) *ISO9000*, Aldershot, Gower.

SCOTT, CYNTHIA D & JAFFE, DENNIS T (1991) *Empowerment: Building a Committed Workforce*, Kogan Page.

SEGALL, L J (1986) 'Integrating Your New Employee into the Organization', *Supervisory Management*, February.

SHEA, GORDON F (1992) *Mentoring: A Guide to the Basics*, Kogan Page.

SMITH, R E (1984) 'Employee Orientation', *Personnel Journal*, December.

STORER, GARY (1990) *Recruiting Young People in the 1990s*, Kogan Page.

SUTTON, R I & LOUIS, M R (1987) 'How Selecting and Socializing Newcomers Influences Insiders', *Human Resource Management*, Vol. 26, No. 3.

TRAINING AGENCY (1987) *It Worked Fine*, (video and) leaflet on managing disabled employees, Moorfoot.

TRAINING AGENCY (1989) *Refugees – Unlocking The Potential*, Training Agency Booklet M128.

TRAINING AND DEVELOPMENT LEAD BODY, *The National Standards for Training and Development*, PO Box 28, Rugby, Warwickshire.

Index

assignments 82
attitudes 86–7
audio-tapes 68–9

benchmarking 115
BS5750/ISO9000 9, 109, 114, 115
business people 34–5

case studies
  benefits of 81
  ineffective induction 13–17
  poor induction programmes
    47–9
Chartermark 115
checklist
  handover 44
  induction 59–60
  planning a training course 123–6
Civil Service department 49
closed question 90
*Code of Practice on the Employment of
  Disabled People* 35
colleagues, role in induction 96–7
communication skills 88–91
contractors 40–1

design of induction, *see* induction
  course; induction training
  programmes
diabetes 35

disabled people 35–6
  Code of Practice on the
    Employment of 35
displays 70–71

employment cycle 99–107
empowerment 113
epilepsy 35
ethnic groups 33
executives, redundant 34–5
exhibitions 70–71
exit interview 18–19, 103–6
ex-offenders 38
ex-service personnel 34

flexible working 31

graduates 38
group discussion 80–81

handouts 84
handover checklists 44
Hertzberg, Frederick 22–3
hierarchy of needs 23
home working 31

individual training programme
    58–9
induction
  checklist 59–60

policy   106–7
review of   60–2, 102–3
induction course   56–8
   design   68, 91–2
   initial   51
   training plan   57–8
induction training
   aims   65–6
   as catalyst for organizational
      change   25–6
   as part of a process   101–2
   'could knows'   64–5
   effects on existing staff   27–8
   financial benefits   17
   in changing environment   26–7
   introducing training and develop-
      ment   25
   learner-centred   68, 79–82
   motivational benefits   21
   'must knows'   64–5
   objectives   66–8
   policy   96
   review   60–2
   'should knows'   64–5
   visual aids   68
induction training programmes
   case studies   47–9
   design   63–75
   methods of delivery   79–85
   model   50–2
   roles in delivery   94–8
   sample course   117–22
induction workbooks   71–2
initial induction course   51
Investors In People (IIP)   9,
      109–10, 113
ISO9000   109, 114, 115

job handovers   43–4
job-sharing   31

knowledge   86–7

leading question   90
leaflets   84

learner-centred methods   68, 79–82
learning organization   113–14
lectures   80
letter of invitation   55–6
listening skills   88
literature   84
local authority   47
Local Enterprise Companies (LECs)
      110
long-term unemployed   32–3

McGregor, Douglas   21–2
management information system   19
managers
   redundant   34–5
   role in induction   95–6
manpower department   95
marathon question   90
Maslow, Abraham   23
mature workers   34
medical problems   35
mentoring   111
mini-induction   53–5
model induction programme   50–2
motivation, theories of   21–4
motivational benefits   21

National and Scottish Vocational
      Qualifications (N/SVQs)
      41–2, 74, 110–11, 113
National standards   72–4
new-entrant scheme   106
newcomers   30–8

observing   89–90
older workers   33–4
open learning   32, 71
open question   91

personnel department   95
photographs   69–70
pre-recruitment training   53
presenting skills   88
pre-visit   50–3
projects   71–2, 82

quality initiatives   114
quality management   115
quality movement   109
questioning   90–1

recruitment
   costs   20
   methods   100–101
   policy   106
redundant managers   34–5
review, of induction training   60–2
review of induction   60–62, 102–3
roles in induction   94–8

S/NVQs   74
school-leavers   36–7
shadowing   84
simulations   82
skills   86–93
slides   69–70
speaking skills   88
special needs   34
staff appraisal   102–3
staff returning from illness   42
staff turnover   17
standards   74–5, 83–4
stress   16
supervisor's role in induction   95–6
syndicate groups   81

tape-slide programmes   70, 81
task analysis   45–6

telecottages   31
teleworking   31
term-time working   31
theories of motivation   21–4
Total Quality Management (TQM)
   109, 114, 115
training and development, new
   approaches in   108–16
Training and Development Lead
   Body (TDLB)   74
Training and Enterprise Councils
   (TECs)   110
training course, checklist for planning   123–6
training cycle   92
training staff   97
two-factor theory   22–3

unemployed   32–3

video programmes   70, 81
visitors   40–1
visual aids   68

waiting lists for induction courses
   55–6
women returners   31
work-based projects   71–2
workbooks   71–2
working abroad   39

X and Y theories   21–2